Diva
-tudes

michelle mckinney hammond

HARVEST HOUSE PUBLISHERS

EUGENE, OREGON

Michelle McKinney Hammond: Published in association with the literary agency of Alive Communications, Inc., 7680 Goddard Street, Ste #200, Colorado Springs, CO 80920.

Cover by Koechel Peterson & Associates, Inc., Minneapolis, Minnesota

Cover image © Simmie Williams

DIVA-TUDES
Copyright © 2005 by Michelle McKinney Hammond
Published by Harvest House Publishers
Eugene, Oregon 97402
www.harvesthousepublishers.com

ISBN-13: 978-0-7369-1549-6
ISBN-10: 0-7369-1549-4

From one diva to another. I dedicate this offering to you the reader because you choose to embrace the courage it takes to effect change in your life. Whether it be a move of inspiration or desperation, whether it be for your own sake or someone who profoundly matters to you, you have just taken the leap required for overcoming and chosen the path that leads to victory—dealing honestly with yourself.

Keep on steppin', my sister; you are almost there!

Acknowledgments

To my Harvest House family, who keeps inspiring me to grow as a writer, teacher, and woman. I soooo love and appreciate you all.

To those who have walked with me and held my arms up to keep me standing. You are the true divas and you know who you are. The list is too long, but one I will mention is my sister Nicole Neal. If only you could see your beauty and the fragrant bouquet you have become. How diva-like of you not to be aware of your own sweet fragrance. But for a moment you should indulge yourself.

Contents

Blessed is the woman who fears God for she will
be covered in favor and blessed by men.

Blessed is the woman who walks in wisdom for
riches, honor, and long life will be hers.

Blessed is the woman who knows she was born
for such a time as this, for she will live her life
with purpose and be fulfilled.

Blessed is the woman who understands she is a
gift to the world for she pursues her destiny
and fulfills it.

Blessed is the woman who is able to celebrate
being a woman for she will enlist the world to
dance with her.

Blessed is the woman who has the right attitude
for the world is hers for the asking.

Divine Wisdom
for
Living, Loving,
and
Overcoming

*G*race and peace be yours in abundance through the knowledge of God and of Jesus our Lord. His divine power has given us everything we need for life and godliness through our knowledge of him who called us by his own glory and goodness. Through these he has given us his very great and precious promises, so that through them you may participate in the divine nature and escape the corruption in the world caused by evil desires. For this very reason, make every effort to add to your faith goodness; and to goodness, knowledge; and to knowledge, self-control; and to self-control, perseverance; and to perseverance, godliness; and to godliness, [sisterly] kindness; and to [sisterly] kindness, love. For if you possess these qualities in increasing measure, they will keep you from being ineffective and unproductive in your knowledge of our Lord Jesus Christ. But if anyone does not have them, [she] is short-sighted and blind, and has forgotten that [she] has been cleansed from [her] past sins. Therefore, my [sisters], be all the more eager to make your calling and election sure. For if you do these things, you will never fall.

2 PETER 1:2-10

An Attitude Adjustment

t's been said time and time again, "Attitude is every-thing"—'tis true, 'tis true. Our thoughts affect our actions. Our actions definitely invite reactions—positive or negative. According to God, we get to choose life or death, blessings or curses, every day. Our actions reveal our choices, and our choices reveal where we really live in our hearts. There-fore, we need to deal with the root of our heart condition in order to implement positive change and get the results we want in every area of our lives.

I don't know about you, but I'm tired of life as usual. I'm tired of crawling over the edges of circumstances, or resigning myself to the thought, "Well, that's just the way things are" or "That's just the way I am." Neither statement is true if we agree with God that we have choices. It's all in the choices we make, ladies. We are the sum total of our attitudes and decisions. Whew! There, I've said it. It's out there now. Can't take it back. Can't blame someone else for where I am. As my good friend Andy Andrews says in one of my favorite reads, *The Traveler's Gift,* the buck stops here. It's called being responsible for my life. Say that out loud with me right now: *I AM RESPONSIBLE FOR MY LIFE.* Now breathe out. We'll never get through this if you don't keep breathing.

I have a confession to make—this devotional was hard for me. Hard because the teacher always becomes the student. So for every question I ask you, I have to answer it myself. Ouch! To be perfectly honest, some things I didn't want to think about or answer. But I so want to grow and be all that God has created me to be. The ultimate for me is putting a big fat grin on His face and hearing Him say, "Yes! Well done!" And knowing that my responsible decision and participation in His plan not only pleased Him, but blessed someone else. So here we go. We are in this thing together.

I assume you bought this book because you were ready to go to the next level of living, loving, and overcoming. This won't happen without some internal work. Some things have to be rearranged. It is time for a spiritual recalibration…so to speak. Our lives are only as transformed as we allow our minds to be renewed. It's time to take a look in the mirror and own some stuff—and *discard* some stuff while we're at it, so we can move forward and get on with the business of living victoriously. We are to have life and have it more abundantly, according to Jesus. *We* should have life, life should not have *us.* Who is running whom here? That is the question, and it's high time you were able to give the right answer. You've got way more dominion over your life than you are exercising. Victory begins in your mind.

Be forewarned. I'm going to give you food for thought and ask you some things about yourself. Now the last time I wrote a book like this, one of my readers filled out everything and mailed the book back to me as if it were a homework assignment. Don't do that. Though I am nosy and would love to know all your business, this is for you, not me. The questions are designed to help you see where you are. This is the same reason God asks us questions. It's not because He doesn't know the answer. He wants you to come to Him and confess where you are in order to effect change in your life. Arriving at your desired destination in a journey requires being specific about where you are presently so you can plot your course accordingly. Make sense?

We are going to take a look in the mirror together. Take off all the makeup and get real about where we are so we can get where we really want to go. Another note here. Because I know we all want to have winning answers and do everything right, I am going to ask you not to take a lot of time to construct your answers. I want you to write down what first comes to mind because that is your truth at the time. This is going to frighten some of you because you are going to say to yourself, "Now I thought I was deeper than that!" It's okay. You can always go back and rewrite anything you want, but you still need to get in touch with the real you before you can know what you need to rearrange. Look at what you've written, and see it for what it is. Don't crucify yourself. See it as a first step toward getting things right.

Our own hearts can scare us when they scream out what's really important to them because intellectually we'd like to think better of ourselves than what our hearts reveal in some instances. That is why we have the Spirit of God alive and well within us. The Spirit makes intercession for us while assisting us in rearranging our heart cries and making the right changes in order for us to reach our full potential. In other words, without the Spirit of God, it is impossible to become the divas we were created to be. All that divahood is just waiting to burst forth from your inner woman, but first you've got to develop the right "diva-tude." Keep it real, my sister.

Remember...your attitude reflects who you really are. And who you are is who you will be until you decide to do the internal work to change your external world and circumstances. "As a woman thinks in her heart, so is she." Mmm, hmm, I thought you knew!

Part 1

Living

MASTERING THE BUSINESS OF LIVING

Understanding is a fountain of life
to those who have it.

PROVERBS 16:22

One

I have come that they might have life,
and have it to the full.

JOHN 10:10

o you have life or does life have you? This is the question you must answer. It is God's intention that you exercise authority over the situations in your life, yet many of us find ourselves overwhelmed and flailing under the circumstances. Losing our grip or feeling out of control, we conclude that it is all too much for us to handle! Anybody been there? Well, my sister, it is time to get a handle on life because that is the correct diva posture. Let's assess the property before we build the house by taking stock of what we've got to work with. Please be honest. This is all *about* you and *for* you. I am giving you permission to focus on yourself, without guilt, so you can be a blessing to many. Are you ready? Go for it girl!

ATTITUDE CHECK

If you could ask God one thing about your life, what would it be?

What do you love about your life?

What don't you like about your life?

What would you like to change about your life? Why?

What is your greatest area of need? Struggle?

What areas have you felt most certain of? Uncertain?

What area of your life has given you the greatest sense of significance?

In what area could you use more growth?

Diva Confession

Today is a new day. The past no longer counts as I create a new present by giving my future to God and agreeing with His divine plan for me. I will begin by _____.

Diva Devotion

Dear heavenly Father, I now confess to You that I have been trying to run my life on my own strength. I have grown so weary from the struggle—a struggle You never intended for me to experience. I choose to rest in Your love, allowing You to pry anything from my grasp that is not my assignment. I now say "yes" to Your will for my life without reservation. Help me to begin again as I place my hand in Yours. Lead me onto the path of Your plan so that I might find the fulfillment I long for in the midst of Your purpose for me. In Jesus' name, amen.

Diva-tude:

BE RICH IN SPIRIT

> A man's [woman's] life does not
> consist in the abundance of
> [her] possessions... Life is more
> than food, and the body
> more than clothes.
>
> LUKE 12:15,23

In your personal opinion, what determines how successful you are in life?

Why are these things significant to you? Are they significant to God? Why or why not?

What things would make you happy even if you did not have a lot of money?

What could you live without?

What could you *not* live without?

Two

So God created man in His own image; in the
image of God He created him; male and female
He created them. Then God blessed them, and
God said to them, "Be fruitful and multiply, fill
the earth and subdue it; have dominion over the
fish of the sea, over the birds of the air, and
over every living thing that moves on the earth."

GENESIS 1:27-28 NKJV

*W*elcome to the rest of your life.
The most liberating fact about life is this: You don't own
anything, not even yourself. As God's creation, you have
been made an administrator, a CEO, a managing partner of
this business called "Your Life."

In order to be successful, every business must have a
plan. The owners must know why it was created—its purpose, what it has to offer, its target market, and how it will
accomplish serving others—to achieve its goals.

The prophet Habakkuk wrote that we should write down
the vision and make it plain in order to be able to run with
it (Habakkuk 2:2). This is called focus. Focus helps you recognize diversions and distractions. It helps you rule out anything that is not conducive to reaching your desired
destination, which in this case, would be the fulfillment of
your destiny. Therefore, the first order of business is to set

your priorities and lay the foundation for prospering in every area of your life by choosing to live purposefully. Don't just think it. Take the time to write it, internalize it, confess it, and live by it.

ATTITUDE CHECK

My Mission Statement

I was created to (do) _____ in order to give (what) _____ to (whom) _____.

Goals

Spiritually: _____.

In order to do this, I must _____

_____.

Relationally: _____.

In order to do this, I must _____

_____.

Physically: _____.

In order to do this, I must _____

_____.

Professionally: _____.

In order to do this, I must _____

_____.

Financially: _____.

In order to do this, I must _____

_____.

My first priority is _____

because _____.

My greatest motivation is _____

_____.

My greatest reward will be _____

_____.

Diva Confession

I can go forth in the assurance that God's plans for my life are certain and true—they will come to pass as I walk in cooperation with Him. In order to receive all that He has for me, I will open my hands and let go of _____
in order to focus on fulfilling what God has created me for and called me to do.

Diva Devotion

Dear heavenly Father, please give me divine focus that not only sees my earthly course, but extends to embrace Your kingdom vision. Thank You for granting me the privilege of being a part of Your amazing plan to bless others as I answer Your call and You meet all my needs. Guide my feet, O God, and steer my heart into the center of Your will for my life. In Jesus' name, amen.

Diva-tude:

BE WISE

> A man's own folly ruins
> his life, yet his heart
> rages against the LORD.
>
> PROVERBS 19:3

What decisions have you made in the past without seeking the Lord? What was the conclusion in each situation?

Why didn't you ask the Lord before making the decisions?

How do you think He would have instructed you differently?

What have you learned from these experiences?

What will you do differently next time?

Three

Who can find a virtuous wife?
For her worth is far above rubies.

PROVERBS 31:10 NKJV

A side from the wife part, how about just who can find a virtuous *woman?* That *virtue* word in this famous text that causes consternation in many a woman can be translated as *capable*. Excellent. In the Hebrew, *chokmah*. That's right. A diva has got to have *chokmah*. She must master the art of skillful living. You see, some skill is required to live this thing called life. That is…if you want to do it right. Let's evaluate some things before we begin.

On a scale of one to ten, with one being "needs improvement," and ten being "I've got this one mastered," how skillfully have you handled the following in your life? (This will help you prioritize where you need to concentrate your efforts.)

_____ Spiritual growth

_____ Relationships

_____ Health

_____ Household

_____ Career

_____ Finances

Now prioritize the above in the order of their importance to you and give the reasons for their placements.

1.

2.

3.

4.

5.

6.

Make a list of what is missing from each of the above-mentioned areas of your life.

Consider the failures as well as the victories you have had in these areas. Based on these prior experiences, write a realistic plan of action for improving each area. Give yourself three steps for each area.

I will look at the entire scope of my life and approach each level of my spirit with the dedication it deserves. I will choose to honor God by being a complete picture of how He created me to function. In order to do this, I will now apply myself to _____

in order to _____.

Dear heavenly Father, I long to be whole, complete, and entire in You. Show me the areas I have ignored and overlooked in my life. Show me how to nurture my spirit and every part of my being so I may be fit to serve and glorify You. Teach me how to live a balanced life that reflects You in Your entirety and brings honor to Your name. In Jesus' name, amen.

Diva-tude:

BE PRUDENT

> Suppose one of you wants to build a tower.
> Will [she] not first sit down and estimate the
> cost to see if [she] has enough money to com-
> plete it? For if [she] lays the foundation and is
> not able to finish it, everyone who sees it will
> ridicule [her], saying, "This [woman] began to
> build and was not able to finish."
>
> LUKE 14:28-30

What is the realistic cost of the things you want to do in your life?

What are you willing to pay to birth your dreams? How much time, resources, and commitment are you willing to sacrifice?

What projects have you started before and not finished? Why not?

What realistic goals can you set today to get on the right track?

Make a 5-day plan. A 30-day plan. A 6-month plan.

Four

The fear of the LORD is
the beginning of knowledge.

PROVERBS 1:7

*I*t all begins and ends here ladies—a healthy dose of respect and fear of the Lord. I recall, as a young woman in high school, observing the behavior of my peers as they made choices that cost them dearly. What separated me from my running buddies was simply this—fear. Fear of getting caught, and greater yet, fear of my *mother*. My mother always had an uncanny way of finding things out. It was even scarier when she predicted things and they happened just as she said. After learning this lesson the hard way, I decided it was best to comply with her rules and save myself the heartbreak of being found out. Or worse yet, of becoming the unwitting victim of the consequences she had forewarned would occur should I choose to go against her instructions.

A healthy respect of my parents' authority was instilled in me at an early age, and I must admit, it kept me out of a lot of trouble. If I scraped up the courage to ask why, I was simply told, "Because I said so." Boy, would that make me mad! But hey, what's a girl to do when she's a child? In hindsight, I came to see the wisdom of my parents' instructions as I compared my life to the stories of those who had chosen to go their own way and revel in their rebellion against authority. Who'da thunk it? Mom and Dad actually knew what they were talking about way back then!

In later years, coming face-to-face with a God who also had rules of conduct to share with me, I found myself once again reflecting on those words, "Because I said so." Was God being mean or just protective? This was what I had to decide. If He truly had good plans for my life, then His instructions were meant for my good, and I should not only respect them, but also *obey* them. If I chose not to, the only person I would hurt would be myself. Actually, in some cases, I would inflict pain on others as well, including the heart of God. But the bottom line is: Even when I don't understand His commands, I must trust His heart toward me. His love and a healthy dose of wisdom will be enough to keep me humble and obey His commands.

ATTITUDE CHECK

What is your attitude toward God?

How do you feel about His commands? What do you feel is His motivation?

On a scale of one to ten, ten being very much, how obedient to God are you in the following areas?

_____Your devotional life

_____Resisting temptation

_____Controlling your tongue

_____Your eating habits

_____Your shopping habits

_____Handling your finances

_____Submitting to authority

_____Taking care of your body

_____Dealing with forgiveness and offense

In which area do you have the most difficulty? Why?

What have been the consequences when you disobeyed God's instructions?

What steps can you take now to gain victory in the areas of self-discipline and obedience?

Diva Confession

I will exercise wisdom by seeing the wisdom of God's commands and adhering to them. I will trust His heart toward me, knowing that He wants me to be the best I can be. In order to cooperate with His plan for my life, I will apply myself toward mastering discipline in the area of _____

_____

in order to gain the lasting benefits of _____

_____.

Diva Devotion

Dear heavenly Father, forgive me for the times I choose to go my own way and give in to what my flesh demands. Help me to yield to Your Spirit more and more each day. I trust You to lead me to the joy and fulfillment I desire so deeply. Most of all, let my ultimate peace and satisfaction come from knowing I have been pleasing to You. In Jesus' name, amen.

Diva-tude:

BE OBEDIENT

> But Samuel replied: "Does the
> LORD delight in burnt offerings and
> sacrifices as much as in obeying
> the voice of the LORD? To obey is
> better than sacrifice, and to heed
> is better than the fat of rams."
>
> 1 SAMUEL 15:22

What fears cause you to take matters into your own hands to get what you desire?

What pressures close in on you to cause you to go against what you know to be true?

What is your response when God does not move in accordance with your timetable on things you desire?

Why do you believe obedience is so important to God? How do you benefit from being obedient to Him?

How does disobedience ultimately rob you of the very thing you desire?

Five

The people that know their God shall be
strong, and do exploits.

DANIEL 11:32 KJV

So here's the real deal. A lot of us know about God,
but do we really *know* Him? Let's face it, we know about a
lot of people, but we don't *knooooow* them. There is a major
difference between knowing *about* and actually *knowing*
someone—feeling his (her) heart, getting in his head, understanding what motivates him. This is huge! It's easy to mis-
interpret the actions or words of someone if you don't really
know his heart. You can't love someone you do not know.
You cannot put your heart and soul into respecting his
wishes if you do not love him. Are you seeing the cyclical
effect here?

We women go through a lot of changes when we are in
love with a man. Loving that man empowers us. It trans-
forms us. It causes us to rearrange priorities, likes and dis-
likes, and even ourselves! Oh...if only we could transfer that
passion to God! What would happen if we did? If we really
got close up and personal with God, got to really, really
know Him, fell deeply in love with Him, and allowed that

love to transform us into incredibly obedient women? We would be empowered to overcome every obstacle in our way. We would walk in such incredible favor we would literally see Red Seas parting in our own lives. The impossible would suddenly be quite possible...every day. Why? Because we would believe Him and follow Him wholeheartedly. This type of behavior can lead you into the center of every miracle you ever dreamed of occurring in your life.

Would you be exempt from trouble? Not by any means. Life happens even for those who love God deeply and do all the right things. However, your response to trials would be different and your power to overcome them more evident than ever. Yes, it's true. The power to overcome and live the type of life you desire comes not from *what* you know, but from *whom* you know.

Sad to say, most of us subconsciously have a "religious" relationship with God. We are so busy studying all the rules and trying to get them right that we forget about the person behind the rules. We never stop to consider why He set these rules in motion. Or, we study the Bible looking for every secret advantage we can apply to our lives, hoping to reap the results of a fulfilling life without regard to the one who knows even more secrets than what is written! Sometimes I think God should feel used...so disregarded. No matter how much He does for us, we are quick to be disappointed when He doesn't line up with what we want. How quickly we forget all He has already done. We're like the children of Israel.

I wonder how many, besides the small crew of Abraham, Jacob, Moses, Joshua, Caleb, and King David (of course there are some more I'm not listing, but you get the idea), were really interested in how God felt about anything. These men drew close to His heart and achieved great things that left an indelible mark in the annals of time. Every diva is aware that how well she knows God will have an effect on all she does and the legacy she leaves behind.

She understands the chain reaction she sets in motion by responding to the heart of God through knowing Him. Knowing Him leads to loving Him. Loving Him leads to wholehearted faith and uncompromising obedience. This type of obedience births extraordinary victories in the lives of those who dare to follow the voice of God.

Are you ready to take this Diva Pop Quiz? You can find some answers in Scripture. Others are conjecture. This quiz is simply designed to give you pause for the cause of getting to know your heavenly Father, the Lover of your soul, and your Mighty Counselor on a more intimate basis. You know… just some things you might not have pondered before. Hopefully these questions will stimulate your curiosity to know more about Him and come up with some questions of your own that provoke you to draw closer, dig deeper, and ultimately see the breadth, depth, and width of God's heart toward you. This revelation should do wonders for your love life and transform your everyday living experience into a happier, more victorious one.

DIVA POP QUIZ

1. What is God's favorite thing to do?

2. What makes God laugh?

3. What makes God weep?

4. What makes God angry?

5. What makes God sad?

6. What is God's favorite color?

7. What is God's favorite scent?

8. What do you think God wants you to know about Him the most?

9. What does God want from us the most?

10. If God could tell you one thing audibly so you never forgot it, what would it be?

Diva Confession

I will make the intimate knowledge of God my chief pursuit, knowing that pursuing His heart is the ultimate source of fulfillment and empowerment. In order to achieve this, I will begin by

_____.

Diva Devotion

Dear heavenly Father, I long to know You in a more intimate way. Draw close and reveal Your heart and mind to me. Show me how to bring a smile to Your face and a song to Your heart. In the midst of my outpourings, refresh and renew my strength to overcome every obstacle I might face as I rest in the complete trust and peace that comes from knowing You. In Jesus' name, amen.

Diva-tude:

BE SINGLE-MINDEDLY "SOUL'D" OUT

No servant can serve two masters.
Either he will hate the one and love
the other, or he will be devoted to
the one and despise the other.

LUKE 16:13

Being truly honest, what do you love and devote yourself
to more than God at this present time?

What will happen if you fail to get the proper perspective
on your desires?

What realities about your desires must you deal with in
order to put God first?

How will putting your priorities and loves in the right order
benefit you in the long run? How will you begin to make
the shift?

What will it take for God to become your first priority?

The LORD rewards every man
for his righteousness and faithfulness.

SAMUEL 26:23

Six

Man does not live on bread alone, but on every
word that comes from the mouth of God.

MATTHEW 4:4

One of my favorite memories of time spent in West
Africa is with a most beloved aunt of mine. Upon waking
in the early morning hours, I found her seated by a table
with a lamp on darning a pair of my uncle's socks. She had
been up for quite a while, already said her morning prayers,
read a devotional along with her Bible for inspiration, and
was now set and centered to begin her day.

After having a delicious breakfast, Auntie Marion and I
set off for the village my uncle was chief of in search of
fish, fresh from the sea, for dinner. By the time we returned,
my uncle had arrived from working in the city. Auntie
Marion had left instructions with the cook for the dinner
menu and everything was served on schedule according to
her precise planning. After a wonderful dinner, we retired
to the study to play card games, sing old hymns, and submit
to my uncle's jesting and teasing. A day could not have been
richer. I could not have been more full of love, peace, joy,
and the fulfillment of a day well spent. That night I said my

prayers and read a verse from my Bible to meditate on in my sleep. I knew what made Auntie Marion so rare and beautiful was the fact she took the time to nurture her own soul before she turned to others. From that year on, the ritual of our Christmas exchange began. From me to her—a brand-new devotional for her to devour during her early morning times of meeting with God. From her to me—one of her beautiful bubuus (they're called caftans here). It's always one she has worn because it isn't just the dress that mattered, I want to take her spirit home and wrap it around me to transport myself back to a serene day with her that I keep hidden in my heart.

From her, I learned it is not the bread we eat, but what our spirit consumes that gives us the ability to nurture others.

ATTITUDE CHECK

How often do you set aside time to nurture your own soul?

What do you do during that time?

What has hindered you from having quality devotional time regularly?

What steps can you take to make this a part of your regular routine?

What would you like your devotional time to look and feel like?

Where can you create a designated sanctuary for yourself?

What will eventually happen if you don't take the time to realign yourself spiritually?

What could a dry and weary spirit cost you in the long run?

Why do you need to apply yourself to making the time to refuel spiritually?

How will this equip you to deal with others? To be a blessing to others?

Diva Confession

I will take the time to invest in the lives of others by first nurturing my own spirit. Out of the abundance of my heart and soul, I will pour out refreshing offerings for those around me. I will begin the discipline of refueling and renewing by applying myself to _____.

Diva Devotion

Dear heavenly Father, forgive me for the times when I have put my day before You and failed to take the time to have the most important meal of the day—the feast of Your Word and Your presence. Help me establish the discipline to make this an integral part of my personal daily ritual. As You fill my cup to overflowing, grant me the precious privilege of refreshing others with what You have given to me. In Jesus' name, amen.

Diva-tude:

BE DISCERNING

> Why spend money on what is not
> bread, and your labor on what does
> not satisfy? Listen, listen to me, and eat
> what is good, and your soul will
> delight in the richest of fare.
>
> ISAIAH 55:2

What things are you pursuing that are not profitable? How are they robbing you of the life you want and the love you need?

What things have you labored over that have not served you well? What will happen if you continue to pursue these things?

What would be good for you right now? What would feed your spirit in a more beneficial way?

What would you have to do to free yourself from the things that are presently holding you back from the satisfaction you crave?

What three steps will you take to begin the process of becoming healthier spiritually? Emotionally?

Seven

And this is love: that we walk
in obedience to his commands.
As you have heard from the beginning,
his command is that you walk in love.

2 JOHN 6

Now let's take a long, slow look at today's verse.
Walking in obedience is not about being a good little "Christian do-bee." It is an active, aggressive display of our love for God. Walking in obedience means walking it out—living it out loud for all the world to witness and not just merely having good intentions. Jesus said very plainly to His disciples, "If you love Me, keep My commandments" (John 14:15 NKJV). That's the love walk. Love that propels us into obedience and submission to God. That is it. In this regard, we can agree that we feel the same way. We believe that others love us when they go out of their way to please us. When they go the extra mile to avoid offending us by sacrificing their own desires, we *really* know they love us! We call it being considerate of our needs. God calls it proof of love.

Love and religion can often be at odds. Religion can be too restrictive—a silent killer of passionate relationships, while love nurtures and kindles the embers in our hearts until a raging fire warms us, drawing others to the light because the loving heart is inviting and contagious. Going through the motions without the emotions (empty religion) feels much like empty intimacy—the type that signals the love affair is over. But to be motivated to obedience by love is to excite the heart of God. Forget the rules, all the thee's and thou's and choose to simply throw yourself into the arms of God—loving Him and serving Him joyously and outrageously. From this place of living, salvation becomes more than just a one-time event—it becomes the promise of an exhilarating future spent with the Lover of your soul. It's obvious you are in love. It's written all over your face and all over your walk. A true diva wears her emotions on more than her sleeve; she wears them on her entire life. Her life becomes a witness to others of what she believes and whom she serves.

ATTITUDE CHECK

What is the motivating factor for the choices you make in life and your everyday situations?

When you consider how God would feel about what you are doing, what is your rationalization for continuing with your choices?

Is your rationalization in line with Scripture? Which verses confirm this? Which verses oppose it?

How can you reconcile what you desire with what God requires?

Why is God's way best in the situation you are tempted by?

What do you think God's laws are designed to do in your life?

What does your obedience or disobedience say to God and others about your relationship with Him?

Diva Confession

Today I will choose to walk in obedience as a passionate gesture of my love for my Lord and King. I will resist the urge to do those things that are not pleasing to Him by remembering _____
_____.

Diva Devotion

Dear heavenly Father, forgive me for the times I chose to love something more than I loved You. Help me have a single-hearted devotion to You. I know there is nothing I can ever do to repay all that You have done for me, but I offer my loving obedience as a sacrifice and gift to You. I love You, Lord. Accept my simple act of worship through obedience as a token of my adoration. In Jesus' name, amen.

Diva-tude:

BE COMPLETELY DEVOTED

> But be very careful to keep the command-
> ment and the law that Moses the servant of
> the LORD gave you: to love the LORD your
> God, to walk in all his ways, to obey his
> commands, to hold fast to him and to serve
> him with all your heart and all your soul.
>
> JOSHUA 22:5

What portion of your heart and soul are you holding back from God?

What would make you give more of yourself to Him? What would be the benefit of doing so?

What boundaries can you set in place to guard your heart and keep you walking in obedience?

When do you struggle with your love for God? What drains your love for God? What increases it?

In what ways do you see the importance of connecting love to obedience?

What would help you be more consistent in your walk with Him?

Eight

[She] who pursues righteousness and love
finds life, prosperity and honor.

PROVERBS 21:21

There they are again. Righteousness and love teamed up as the dynamic duo for nurturing your spirit and gaining what externally as well as internally? Life, prosperity, and honor...I'll take those, won't you? That pretty much sums up what everyone wants. *Life* in the context used here is more than just existing. It speaks to living well here and forevermore. Life at its fullest and richest—right standing with God, which leads to possessing the type of peace and joy that cannot be affected by outer circumstances.

A healthy spirit breeds integrity and sound character, which leads to honor because others take note of the quality of your life, actions, and relationships. Ultimately, a life of prosperity is the overflow of a life well lived—not just materially, but emotionally and spiritually. Recently, I was at an event where a man who was well loved by his peers rose to speak. They were all there to honor him for his contributions to those who were less fortunate than himself. The ticket price had been high for a seat at this banquet, and yet the hall was filled. He said he was humbled by the showing and found it hard to believe that so many people had been diverted from their busy lives in the middle of the week to pay so much money to come and join him for dinner. He ended by saying he was a wealthy man because of his friends. How true, how true!

Perhaps far too many people have put the cart before the horse by pursuing prosperity and honor first. They have been settling for the crumbs of life instead of feasting at the banquet table God wants to provide when we simply pursue right standing with Him first. Every diva knows that the proof of her prosperity does not lie in her bank account or the multitude of her possessions, but in the lives of those who have chosen to walk with her in love as partners and friends through this awesome journey called life. This wealth is not acquired by osmosis. It is not maintained by wit and charm. It grows and flourishes via the work that it takes to nurture and cultivate continuous growth. It is contingent not on what others do for you, but what you do for others.

We are told to *pursue* righteousness and love. Sometimes that seems like such hard work, but it has a payoff worth working for. Pursue righteousness because it will work for you. Doing the right thing always does. Pursue love because it will not run from you. It is infectious, catching the most resistant off guard. Remember that God pursued us. That is what love does. It cannot stand to live for itself. Love must reach out and touch someone else, catch someone else and hold them in its embrace. You will never feel more alive than when you are passionately in love. If not *in* love, just loving to your fullest potential. At the end of the day, to be held and possessed by love is the richest experience of all because this is where life begins and ends.

ATTITUDE CHECK

Name your top five pursuits in the order of their importance to you.

1.

2.

3.

4.

5.

Has this order garnered the results you want in your life?

How can you actively pursue righteousness? Love?

What holds you back from these pursuits?

How can you overcome these hindrances? Why would it benefit you to overcome them?

Up to this point, in what areas of life have you felt robbed?

How can pursuing righteousness and love fulfill these areas?

Diva Confession

Today I will actively take responsibility for acquiring the life I want by pursuing righteousness and love. In order to do this, I will free myself from the following hindering thoughts and actions: _____.

Diva Devotion

Dear heavenly Father, today I choose to roll up my sleeves and do the work it takes to have the life You desire for me and I desire for myself. I will actively and passionately pursue righteousness and love at all costs, keeping my eye on the prize that lies in store for me. Make me a wise steward of the life, honor, and prosperity You bestow on those who run after your heart first and foremost. In Jesus' name, amen.

Diva-tude:

BE KINGDOM-MINDED

> Seek ye first the kingdom of
> God, and his righteousness;
> and all these things shall be
> added unto you.
>
> MATTHEW 6:33 KJV

Describe the perfect kingdom—God's kingdom. How does it operate? What are the benefits to its citizens?

How can you pursue kingdom living now?

How does kingdom living affect your present lifestyle?

What are the benefits of righteousness, of being right with God?

How does righteousness affect you mentally? Physically? Emotionally?

Nine

Therefore be clear minded and self-controlled
so that you can pray.

1 PETER 4:7

The greatest killers of intimacy with God and others are guilt, anger, shame, and fear. We, like Adam after his fatal bad choice in the garden, panic when we know we've blown it and run for cover. But part of communication is being clear on where we are and being honest about it. Guilt and shame cloud the issue and shut down communication. The disciple Peter, later named an apostle, knew this. When he addressed the church, he was writing to encourage them to be sober and clear about why they were following God and to make responsible choices from a place of discipline and self-control so that nothing could stand between them and God.

It is the daily choices we make that determine our level of intimacy with God. The right choices, those that please our heavenly Father, keep us in right-standing with Him. These choices lead to peace because we are free from guilt and have the joy that comes from living expectantly because we are on good terms with God, so much so that the Holy

Spirit abides with us, encouraging and counseling us along the way. His instructions are not diffused by the unresolved issues of guilt from poor choices, such as the fear that God is not pleased with us, the shame from not getting a handle on ourselves or our lives, or the anger that can be directed at ourselves or God when we feel we've endured one disappointment too many (even if we did play a part in the outcome of the situation).

If we keep in mind that prayer is a conversation, let's consider that one of the killers of a satisfying exchange is offense. If either of the parties is unhappy with the actions or words of the other, the conversation is strained...that is, if any conversation takes place at all! The same is true with God. It is difficult to pray if we feel our prayers are bouncing off the ceiling. It is only when our conscience is clear that we are able to be uninhibited when approaching the Throne Room. It is under this open heaven that we are able to give of ourselves freely, anticipating the pleasure and participation of the Lover of our souls in this most intimate conversation.

ATTITUDE CHECK

What would you like to improve about your prayer life?

What are the greatest distractions or hindrances to your prayers?

How does guilt affect your prayer life? Fear? Shame? Anger?

What type of disciplines do you need to apply to your prayer life to make it a richer time?

Make a list of things you have avoided talking to God about and why.

What would you like to see occur during your prayer time? What do you need to do to make this a reality?

Diva Confession

I will make quality choices concerning my conduct in order to pursue peace with God and a quality relationship with Him. In order to enhance my prayer life, I will _____.

Diva Devotion

Dear heavenly Father, forgive me for withdrawing when I should be seeking You. Due to my own poor choices at times, my guilt and shame have needlessly separated me from You. Today I purpose that this moment will be a new beginning for us. Help me to make right choices and enjoy sweet times of fellowship with You from this day forward. In Jesus' name, amen.

Diva-tude:

BE PRAYER-FULL

> And when you pray, do not keep
> on babbling like pagans, for they
> think they will be heard because
> of their many words.
>
> MATTHEW 6:7

How much time do you spend talking *at* God? Listening?

Do you approach God as a loving Father or a harsh Judge?
How do you feel when you are praying?

How much of your prayer time is spent on your own issues?
On others? On reflecting on God's Word?

What adjustments need to be made based on your previous
answer?

Set aside a time to have an intimate date with the Lord. You can be as creative as you like in the time you spend together. Your date must last for two hours, and you must be silent for one hour. Write what occurs or what you hear during that time.

Ten

But you, dear friends, build yourselves up in
your most holy faith and pray in the Holy Spirit.

JUDE 20

Our relationship with God is not a one-shot deal. Life happens and there are events that can sometimes rock our faith. The first infusion of faith we receive upon salvation must be nurtured and maintained. It must be built upon. Just as the body needs food for nourishment and the building up of cells and muscle, our spirits crave the bread of God for sustenance and strength. How do we go about this? By maintaining open communication with the Keeper of our souls. His loving promises, wise instructions, and reassurances of His faithfulness to us are the things that cause us to rest secure within the house of faith.

Jesus knew the necessity of spending quality time with the Father. He sought Him out first thing in the morning. It was a time of communion, of sharing from the heart, of listening to the one who, in all of His omniscience, leaned down from heaven to give Jesus insight, understanding, and instructions for the day. In the evening, Jesus crept away again to debrief in a sense. By doing it this way, I believe

Jesus kept short accounts of anything that troubled Him, any issues that weighed heavy on His heart concerning His assignment on earth or even His various interactions with those who were clueless about His mission or identity. It was during this time of exchange that God gave Him great and precious promises that sustained Him through all He endured.

And so it is with us. As we take the time to steal away for our own personal communion, the Holy Spirit meets us in that quiet place. And He who searches the heart and knows the mind of God makes intercession for us when we don't know how to pray for ourselves. Even when it's in groans that cannot be uttered, God knows and comprehends the language of the Spirit and is faithful to meet us and answer our prayers.

During this time, God reveals Himself to us through an inner knowing in our spirit. Perhaps it can be through a scripture that comes alive to us or simply a quiet assurance that all is well. Whichever way God chooses to meet us, the tower of our faith grows stronger and becomes a haven for others to visit during times of doubt and wonderment.

ATTITUDE CHECK

What drains you of your faith? What builds it up?

How do you handle things when you are doubtful or fearful?

What outlets do you seek when your faith is unstable?

How long do you continue to wrestle with your fears in your own strength? What is the outcome of dealing with life in this manner?

What hinders you from praying when you are anxious?

What do you need to do to break through the paralysis and seek God?

Diva Confession

I will nurture consistency in my walk by taking the time to feed my spirit and build up my faith by _____.

Diva Devotion

Dear heavenly Father, Bread of heaven, please feed me. Fill me with Yourself and nourish my heart. Saturate me with Your faithful instruction. Build me up in my most holy faith that I may be a vessel of honor for You. Strengthen me, sustain me, and use me for Your glory. In Jesus' name, amen.

Diva-tude:

BE AN INTERCESSOR

> And pray in the Spirit on all
> occasions with all kinds of
> prayers and requests. With this in
> mind, be alert and always keep
> on praying for all the saints.
>
> EPHESIANS 6:18

How free are you when it comes to requesting things from God?

How much of your prayer life is spent in thanksgiving and worship?

What types of things do you ask for when you pray?

How often do you pray for others? What distracts you from praying for others?

Do you have a prayer partner? Get one if you don't have one. Covenant to pray together once a week at a set time. Keep a log of your prayers and the answers to them.

Diva Inventory

On a scale of one to ten, with ten being great, how are you doing in these areas? How can you improve?

____Wealth in the spirit

____Wisdom

____Prudence

____Obedience

____Focus

____Discernment

____Devotion—to God, to others

____Kingdom vision

____Intimacy with God

____Burden for others

Part 2

Loving

REALIZING THE POWER OF LOVE

Everyone who loves is born of God
and knows God.

1 JOHN 4:7

Getting a Love Life

Keep your heart with all diligence,
for out of it spring the issues of life.

PROVERBS 4:23 NKJV

The big question to ask is not just how are you living, but also how are you loving? How you are loving will have a lot to do with how you are living. The way you feel about God and yourself will affect how you relate to others. The difficulties we experience in relationship to others will always lead back to us in the end. We have our part in the drama, no matter how much we feel like the victim. Ooh, a bunch of folks just got really indignant. But the reality is...what I said is true.

Whether you did nothing more than choose to open yourself up to someone and miss every warning sign that something was wrong, or you submitted yourself to needless abuse just to have a job or a relationship, you have a part in your circumstance. It can be as simple as not asking the right questions in the beginning or not listening to the people who love you. It could be allowing the situation to go unconfronted and unchecked the first time it happened or being too consumed with your own issues and needs to see that they were leading you to a place of deeper wounding. Shall I go on?

Love is deep. Who can figure it out? We all want it, need it, are fascinated by it, scared of it, hate it, and love, love, love it. Why is love always an issue? Because we were created to love. We've got to do it. Nothing else in life will ever be enough to drown out the natural craving of the heart or fill the spiritual void that God created within us specifically for the function of loving.

I participated in a discussion panel recently on the topic of love and relationships, and a member of the audience rose to her feet to ask a very simple question: "What is love?" No one on the panel responded. The same people who had so much to say earlier were loudly silent. Finally, I spoke up and said, "Love is giving everything you have for the benefit of the one you love."

You see, that is what God did. God so loved the world that He gave His one and only Son (John 3:16).

If we look at the "love chapter" (1 Corinthians 13), there is nothing there about what you get. It's all about giving! Love is not about you; it's about the other person! The greatest secret to getting what you want is being willing to give it away. Oh my...no wonder we have so much trouble with love.

Think about it. If everyone was caught up in giving to someone, everyone would feel loved. Unfortunately, we have a lot of people spending more time holding their love for ransom based on what people do for them or give them. Bartering for hearts is not God's idea of love. Love will cost you everything if you are doing it right, but in return, you will gain more than you ever give. Not because you demand or require it, but because when you dare to love like God, it opens the floodgates for you to receive the love you long for. Remember, we were made not only to love but to respond to love as well. We love God because He first loved us; therefore, we can never love too much. Don't confuse that with spoiling others or being a victim of someone who lacks the understanding of what true love is. I am merely speaking of loving from the heart. A heart filled with love is a healthy heart. Only when other things such as feelings of entitlement, unforgiveness, fear, bitterness, resentment, envy, and jealousy occur do we grow sick and stop being whole because we have bought into the deception that we need more than what we originally had in order to possess peace and joy.

It is at this point, when we foolishly believe God is holding out on us, that we find ourselves back in the garden with Eve under the curse, striving for someone else to fill the void in our hearts in a manner he or she was never created to. Unrealistic expectations cause us to establish rules in our hearts that make it difficult for us to achieve getting the love we want. The problem with our personal rules for love and fulfillment is that usually other people don't know about them. *Aaaaannnd,* they have their own set of rules! So now you're expecting someone else to live up to your love rules, but that person is living and loving according to his or her own rules. Oh, brother! Or should I say sister? This can really complicate matters of the heart, but hopefully, as the light goes on, you will free yourself up from these rules and receive more love than you thought possible.

Eleven

Love the LORD your God with all your heart and
with all your soul, and with all your strength.

DEUTERONOMY 6:5

The foundation of all other loves is your love affair
with God. The reason I call it a love affair is because it
should not be a "religious" experience. Your relationship
and interaction with God should have all the love, excitement, and passion you've always longed for in your other
earthly relationships. Look at it this way—with God you get
to participate in communication, honesty, transparency,
giving, and vulnerability without the fear of rejection. He
will always love you; He will never leave or forsake you.
Your heart is completely safe with Him.

God epitomizes love because He *is* love. He, being love,
is the ultimate authority and expert on how love operates.
So let's take a look at what love means to Him. We know
that He loved us so much that He gave—He gave the
greatest sacrifice of all, the thing nearest and dearest to Him,
His Son, Jesus Christ. Then on top of that, in spite of massive rejection, He keeps reaching out to us. In the face of

our total disregard of His feelings as we go our own way at times, blatantly disobeying His wishes, He forgives and restores us. Not once, not twice, not three strikes you're out, but again and again. His love is purely unconditional.

However, He has set healthy boundaries and conditions for having and maintaining a relationship with Him. Accept His gift of love. Stay in honest and open communication. Be willing to face, own, and confess wrongs and offenses against Him. Joyfully serve Him. Listen to His heart and Word and follow His directions. Love what He loves. Make Him look good and introduce Him to others. This is a reasonable list of expectations in light of all He has done for us. As a matter of fact, if we did all of this consistently, we would still owe Him big time! He always remains faithful to us—supplying our needs, loving and protecting us in the middle of more dumb choices than we care to think about.

Loving God with all our heart, soul, mind, and strength puts us on automatic pilot for doing the right thing toward others because part of loving Him includes loving others properly. It's all connected, ladies. The heart is the engine that drives the mind and soul to line up and follow suit with its decisions. Our will is also tied to the amount of energy we exert toward our commitments. Loving God will not always be a warm and fuzzy experience, but it is a commitment just the same. True love remains constant to the commitment even when emotions don't line up. You must keep going and do the work it takes to reignite the flame. Trust me, if you cannot reach consistency in your relationship with God, who is the easiest person on the planet to love because He is perfect, consider what that says about how you will fare in your earthly relationships. A true diva knows to build the foundation for loving on solid ground. Divas put first things first—loving God.

ATTITUDE CHECK

If you were talking about God as the love of your life to a friend, how would you describe Him?

What do you like about God? Why? What do you *not* like about God? Why?

Is your perception of God true or based on emotion?

What would you like your relationship with God to be like?

What is keeping you from having the type of relationship with God you would like?

How will you begin to nurture the type of relationship you want with Him?

Diva Confession

I will no longer live in my head in my relationship with God. I will pursue and love Him with a passionate heart that overflows with adoration and gratefulness for all that He has done for me. I will begin today by_____.

Diva Devotion

Dear heavenly Father, I so long to love You the way You long to be loved by me. Fill my heart with Your love. Let my heart beat in harmony with Yours. Help me hear Your heart and respond to it. Take me past the fear of loving with abandon and give me the courage to love the way You do. In Jesus' name, amen.

Diva-tude:

BE OBEDIENT

> Whoever has my commands and
> obeys them, he is the one who
> loves me. He who loves me will be
> loved by my Father, and I too will
> love him and show myself to him.
>
> JOHN 14:21

What is the greatest way you can prove your love for God?

What prompts God to bless us?

Why does God desire our obedience?

Who do we really hurt when we are disobedient?

How does your obedience defeat the enemy?

Twelve

To love your neighbor as yourself is more
important than all burnt offerings and sacrifices.

MARK 12:33

*P*erhaps today's verse reveals where the trouble begins.
It is hard to celebrate others if we don't feel good about
ourselves. The sin of comparison sets in, making us critical
and bitter toward others, unable to celebrate the things
about them we should. We become resistant to being gen-
uinely loving toward them and happy for their blessings and
accomplishments.

What exactly does God mean by loving yourself anyway?
I mean, isn't that considered selfish if you are really a good
Christian? There's a thin line between not loving our lives
to the death and loving ourselves in a healthy, whole
manner. *Aren't we supposed to be more concerned about
others, Michelle?* Well God said it, I didn't. "Love your
neighbor as yourself." Obviously some loving of yourself
has to happen here in order to be able to love your
neighbor. Jesus took it even further by suggesting that if we
could master the first two commandments, this one and
loving God totally, we would automatically fulfill all the

other commandments (which I hope you know are more
than ten!). Could this be the key to doing the right thing in
every circumstance, causing us to forego the things that
wound and hurt others?

I believe that loving your neighbor as yourself is a
twofold command. I don't think we are supposed to spend
a lot of time dwelling on ourselves, but some things need
to be established until they just "are," they're a part of our
being. We must respect the self we are because we are a
temple of the Holy Spirit. The house that God lives in on
earth. If you've ever seen any photos of a king's palace, it
is a beautiful, well-kept place. No graffiti and no junk or
garbage lying around. Everything is spotless—clean and
beautifully cultivated and cared for. It leaves its visitors in
awe. The very surroundings indicate that someone of great
importance lives there. We will get into this a little deeper
later on. Stay with me, I'm taking this somewhere.

When God created you, He uttered the same words He
said long ago at the beginning of time: "It is good." How do
I know that? Because everything God creates is good. It is
good enough for what He created it to do. Therefore, it is perfect. That means you are perfect. Perfect for what God had
in mind when He created you. So stop with all the compar-
isons and questions. Am I tall enough, good enough, lovable
enough, good enough, smart enough, good enough, thin
enough, good enough, pretty enough, good enough? Enough
already! Indeed you are.

By now you should have guessed the second half of the
command—turn your attention toward treating others the
way you would want to be treated yourself, with patience,
kindness, trust, consideration…you know the whole list.
Divas are free to do exactly that because they are practicing
this command with themselves.

ATTITUDE CHECK

How do you regard yourself?

How does this translate into how you deal with others?

What is the connection between your insecurities and your responses toward others?

Does your present attitude help you cultivate the type of relationships with others you would like?

List five good things about yourself.

1.

2.

3.

4.

5.

How would God want to use those things to bless others?

Diva Confession

I will celebrate the fact that I was created as I am, on purpose, to be a source of blessing to others by being a conduit of God's love to them. I will nurture my own heart by _____, thus making myself a greater vessel of nurturing for others.

Diva Devotion

Dear heavenly Father, I will bless You by being grateful for the way You created me. I will no longer question Your handiwork or magnify my imagined shortcomings. I will instead choose to focus on my areas of strength and how I can use them to be a greater vessel of blessing to others. Thank You for the privilege of being able to be a channel of Your love. In Jesus' name, amen.

Diva-tude:

BE FORGIVING

> But I tell you who hear me: Love your ene-
> mies, do good to those who hate you....If
> you love those who love you, what credit
> is that to you? Even "sinners" love those
> who love them....But love your enemies,
> do good to them, and lend to them
> without expecting to get anything back.
> Then your reward will be great, and you
> will be sons of the Most High, because he
> is kind to the ungrateful and wicked.
>
> LUKE 6:27,32,35

What is your first response to those who offend you?

Is everyone you know aware of your personal rules for how you should be treated? Should those who don't be held responsible?

How easy is it for you to forgive? In what ways do you struggle to release offense once it occurs?

What road map can you write for yourself to ensure an easier transition from offense to forgiveness?

Who is it easier for you to forgive—family, friends, or strangers? Why? What is the difference? Is that a fair differentiation?

In what ways might the other people be struggling? Are they aware that they offended you?

How will the quality of your life be affected if you don't release them in forgiveness?

Thirteen

He who covers over an offense promotes love,
but whoever repeats the matter
separates close friends.

PROVERBS 17:9

There is a popular saying that states the three quickest modes of communication are telephone, telegraph, and tell a woman. Not cute. However, we must admit that we tend to delight in nursing and rehearsing situations that have caused us dismay, hurt, or drama. How many conversations have you begun with the sentence, "Don't repeat this, but..."? Mmm hmm, probably too many to remember. Ironically, this little disclaimer usually does not ensure that your request will be honored. Before it was over, more people were hurt as the matter was discussed among others. Even if those who repeated the issue were not malicious in their intent, the situation took a turn for the worse. It could have been simply handled between the two parties involved without the heightened emotions of feeling betrayed or exposed even further.

What is the model for reconciliation in circumstances such as these? Scripture is very clear. We are to go to our sisters (or brothers) and let them know how they have offended us. If they show no signs of remorse, then we are to go to the elders in the church and have them mediate the matter. If elders are not available in a church, I suggest someone who is a mature and grounded Christian with good people skills and a heart bent toward reconciliation.

The quickest way to blow a disagreement out of proportion is to repeat it to all who will listen, sometimes causing irreparable damage. I dare say that when this happens, we might protest a bit too much. Either we played a bigger part in the offense than we are willing to admit at the time or we are searching for an answer as to why it happened in the first place. Might I suggest the answer to this lies with the person who committed the offense?

God does not hang our dirty laundry out to dry. He confronts us in private and calls us to be reconciled to Himself. Notice the end goal: Reconciliation. When Adam and Eve sinned in the garden, God confronted them in love. Though Adam was not readily willing to confess his sin, God made a sacrifice and covered him and Eve. He was more interested in salvaging their relationship than pointing a finger in blame. Every diva knows the secret to mending broken bridges is not to publicize them. Quietly take out your tools and do the work it takes to close the gap.

ATTITUDE CHECK

What is your reaction when you have been offended?

How easily do you repeat a matter? What are the results?

How easy is it for you to discuss the offense with the one who offended you?

In what ways can you be the conduit of reconciliation?

What steps can you take to resist unforgiveness, resentment, and blame?

Diva Confession

From this day forward, I will operate from a place of love no matter what someone does to me. I will not readily repeat a matter that causes me offense. Instead, I will _____.

Diva Devotion

Dear heavenly Father, forgive me for the times I have not exhibited the same compassion toward others that You have shown to me. Teach me how to live in love and reflect Your heart to others, even when they offend me. Help me look beyond the fault and see their need or see my own need arising out of the pressure that is created from the offense. Teach me to embrace the lesson, even greater yet, to embrace my offender. In Jesus' name, amen.

Diva-tude:

BE MERCIFUL

> Because of the LORD's great love
> we are not consumed, for his
> compassions never fail.
>
> LAMENTATIONS 3:22

What things have you done where you felt undeserving of God's love?

How did you respond to His mercy when He extended it to you?

In what instances have you prayed for compassion from others?

In what circumstances was the offense you were accused of a matter of misunderstanding?

How much of your offender's behavior really had to do with you or another problem they may be experiencing? How can you tell?

Fourteen

But God demonstrates his own
love for us in this: While we were
still sinners, Christ died for us.

ROMANS 5:8

*I*t's one thing to talk the talk, but it is another thing to *walk* the talk. As I travel the country talking to many desperate singles and disappointed married people, I see one common unrealistic expectation. The need for someone else to be their validation. When I ask singles, "What do you have to give to the mate you are seeking?" they grow strangely silent. Of course, they were looking for someone to fill them up! When I ask the dissatisfied married person, "What have you poured into your mate lately that gave you joy in the giving?" I get the same silence. *Hmm, but this isn't about me giving, Michelle. It's about what I'm not getting!*

Sorry to burst your bubble, but love is more about giving...and even more about dying. Yes, dying to your preconceived notions about what you are supposed to get. Dying to what you want and your own personal agenda. Dying to the expectations that love is the end all for true happiness. Consider this thought: God did what was painful to win us. In the pouring out, we were drawn to Him...and

He ultimately gains what He wants—our hearts—but not without losing everything first.

Divas know that the greatest gains are made in return for the greatest sacrifice. They give no thought to what they are losing, choosing instead to focus on the outcome—a life of abundant joy and fulfillment that can only come from losing themselves in the process of giving and loving.

ATTITUDE CHECK

What makes you feel loved?

What do you do to make others feel loved?

How much joy do you get from giving? Why?

Where does your joy come from in your relationships?

What could you give more of in your relationships?

How much are you willing to give if you don't get what you want in return?

How will you reconcile your desires with what God requires?

Diva Confession

Today I choose to change my definition of love to agree with God's heart. Instead of expecting _____ from others, I will purpose instead to _____.

Diva Devotion

Dear heavenly Father, make my heart more like Yours. Teach me how to give outrageously and joyously without seeking anything in return. Let receiving cease to be my motivation. Allow the privilege of giving to be my greatest reward knowing that as I pour out my love in accordance with Your plan, all I long for will be given to me as You honor my obedience to You. In Jesus' precious name, amen.

Diva-tude:
BE AUTHENTIC

> Love must be sincere....Be
> devoted to one another
> in [sisterly] love. Honor one
> another above yourselves.
>
> ROMANS 12:9-10

What motivates you to do kind things for others?

What is the acid test of love for you? What must someone do to prove his or her love to you?

Are you able to be at your best when your loved one is not?

What are some ways that you can honor your loved ones above yourself?

How can you be a true sister to the men (mate excluded) in your life?

Fifteen

Love is patient, love is kind. It does not envy,
it does not boast, it is not proud. It is not rude,
it is not self-seeking, it is not easily angered,
it keeps no record of wrongs. Love does not
delight in evil but rejoices with the truth.
It always protects, always trusts, always hopes,
always perseveres. Love never fails.

1 CORINTHIANS 13:4-8

oday's verses include quite a laundry list, don't they? Most of you are thinking right now, *Can I go for two out of sixteen?* The answer is no. We must conquer them all. Every diva saturates herself in the understanding of how love operates and masters the disciplines of love. They actually feed into one another. Love can be patient because it always hopes for the best to come from the other person. It trusts even when one is being unlovable, they persevere, being kind until the loved one is able to rise above whatever is disrupting her true nature. Love is not easily angered because it is not thinking about itself first. It has no sense of rights being violated because it is not interested in keeping a list of the beloved's failures.

When we love, we strive to protect our loved ones from

hurt because we would not delight in watching them being wounded or falling prey to evil. Therefore, we seek out the root of what is going on with the other people and rejoice in shedding light and truth that will set the others free. Love is so devoted to the beloved that it does not allow pride to make it give up even when the going gets tough. It doesn't feel the need to boast about its exploits, nor does it envy or grow intimidated by successes or possessions. Love just loves, and keeps on loving, no matter what. Whew!

How does this play out in the lives of everyday divas? Well, if you're single, you can love a brother even if he is not your husband. If you are a wife, you can love your husband even when he is not being the man you fell in love with. As single or married women, the greatest power we possess over a man is the power to love. The greatest power we have to wield in the world at-large is the power of love. God invented love. Love overcomes evil. Not getting the response you want? Love anyway. Through the eyes of love see those in front of you rising up to the full stature of what God would have them become. Be an instrument of inspiration, a cheerleader, because the power of love fuels your faith to believe the very best will be manifested in the lives of everyone your love touches.

Go ahead, love people into fruitfulness. Love them into purposefulness. Love them into being all that God created them to be. Love them into being more loving! Yes, that's right. The secret lies in the recesses of your own heart. Love never fails.

ATTITUDE CHECK

On a scale of one to ten, rate the following according to your greatest strength/weakness in exercising love with those in your life intimately and socially.

Love Attribute	Intimate Relationships (mate or family)	Socially (friends or co-workers)
Patience	_____	_____
Kindness	_____	_____
Envy	_____	_____
Boasting	_____	_____
Pride	_____	_____
Consideration	_____	_____
Anger	_____	_____
Record Keeping of Offenses	_____	_____
Bitterness	_____	_____
Selfishness	_____	_____
Protecting the Other	_____	_____
Trust	_____	_____
Optimism	_____	_____
Perseverance	_____	_____

Compare the strengths and weaknesses between your intimate inner circle and those you interact with in more social situations. What does this reveal?

What are we trying to protect when we don't give ourselves as we should?

What decisions can you make in order for your love flow to be uninterrupted, no matter what the responses of others appear to be?

Diva Confession

Today I will take the lead by being a conductor of love. I will be the flint that ignites the spark in the heart of others by being more _____ _____. I will begin by _____.

Diva Devotion

Dear heavenly Father, I confess that so much of what I do in the name of love is conditional. Teach me how to love like You. Allow me to always trust You to keep my heart as I hope for the best in others and cheer them on to that end by extending my love to them, even when the return looks doubtful. Thank You, Lord, for Your love that never stops believing in me. In Jesus' name, amen.

Diva-tude:

BE WHAT YOU PREACH

If I speak in the tongues of men and of angels, but have
not love, I am only a resounding gong or a clanging
cymbal. If I have the gift of prophecy and can fathom all
mysteries and all knowledge, and if I have a faith that can
move mountains, but have not love, I am nothing. If I
give all I possess to the poor and surrender my body to
the flames, but have not love, I gain nothing.

1 CORINTHIANS 13:1-3

If you were arrested for being loving, what evidence would
be used against you in a court of law?

Which disciplines from 1 Corinthians 13:4-8 are you strong
in?

Which disciplines do you need to work on? Which ones are
more difficult for you? Why?

Which one hinders your love flow the most? How will you
reconcile this area of your life?

Write a mission statement for yourself concerning your new
attitude toward being more loving.

And now these three remain: faith, hope and
love. But the greatest of these is love.

1 CORINTHIANS 13:13

Sixteen

Do everything in love.

1 CORINTHIANS 16:14

hat is my motivation?" is a famous line from those getting ready to act out a difficult scene in a movie or play. They must pick a focus, a reason to respond in the manner prescribed in the manuscript.

Having a reason to be loving as directed by God's manuscript helps. Having background on the situation helps. Sometimes love can be a difficult scene. At times you need a reason to love in spite of the other person. Let's start with the basics. If you walk in love, allowing love to be your motivation for everything you do, you will have peace—the peace of knowing you did your best and gave your all. If the other people couldn't deal with it, hey that was on them. Perhaps they just weren't ready for prime time. You, however, starred in your role. After peace, joy would be a close second. There is joy in knowing you had something to give, and you gave it with abandon. It felt good when you were doing it, and it feels even better when you look back and view your handiwork. These are but two of the priceless rewards for loving. Favor, more love, sound relationships, and personal growth are just a few more.

But beyond what you will get out of it, there is the effect of what your actions will mean to others—how they will affect others, and so on. But ultimately, it comes down to the way you will be viewed and rewarded by God. What we sow is what we reap. If you sow love, whether someone can give it back or receive it properly is not the issue, your return will ultimately be based on what you did. Love overpowers evil and emotional paralysis, as well as all the other things that could be a hindrance to you flowing freely and generously toward others. Love breaks down walls that have been erected in the name of past hurts, fears, misgivings...you name it. If we sow sparingly, we are told we will reap sparingly, but a flood of love sown where resistance is at its most determined will reap the power of overcoming opposition and obtaining victory in the most difficult of circumstances and relationships.

Check your motivation. Simply to love...not to get anything...will save you immense heartache. To love for the sake of loving is the ultimate in freedom. You are no longer bound by others' responses. A diva does not allow anyone to rule her emotions or her capacity to love. She is fearless with her heart knowing that God is the Keeper of it. As she allows His love to flow to even the most unlovable, she gets back more than she ever expected. And does so without having to ask for it!

ATTITUDE CHECK

How driven are you to perform for love? What happens when you don't receive the response you desire?

When it comes to feeling loved, how difficult do you make it for yourself to achieve that feeling?

What conditions or expectations hinder you from being freer in this area?

What attitude can you adopt toward loving and giving that will stop you from being "the victim"?

What is the best way to get your need for love met?

Diva Confession

Today I will regain the power of love in my life by changing my attitude toward loving. I will begin by changing my motivation for why I _____. From now on, I will _____.

Diva Devotion

Dear heavenly Father, make my heart more like Yours. Teach me to have the courage to love regardless of others' inability to do so. Help me to sow gardens of love wherever I am planted and to produce sweet fruit that is, above all things, pleasing to You. In Jesus' name, amen.

Diva-tude:

BE FRUITFUL

Be completely humble and
gentle; be patient, bearing with
one another in love.

EPHESIANS 4:2

How much do you struggle with pride when assessing how much of yourself to give to another?

How can it be an aggressive course of action to humble yourself to another?

What is the power of being gentle? Why is strength required in order to be patient? How can you utilize more of both?

In which area do you struggle the most in your significant relationship: humility, gentleness, or patience? What causes you to respond in an opposite fashion?

Write out a plan of action for yourself on how exercising the attributes of love will deepen or improve your relationship. Give yourself five steps to begin to practice.

1.

2.

3.

4.

5.

Seventeen

However, each one of you also must love his
wife as he loves himself, and the wife must
respect her husband.

EPHESIANS 5:33

an we talk about the role that respect plays in the
love arena? Why didn't God tell the woman to love the man?
That seems to be the obvious exchange, doesn't it? An eye
for an eye, love for love...seems fair. Yet God specifically
commands the man to love the woman. The woman is commanded to *respect* her husband, yet she must be *taught* how
to love her husband by an older mentor. Hmm...interesting.
Could it be that a man's definition of love is different from
a woman's? Absolutely.

We women operate on the premise that to be loved is
to be cared for. However, you cannot expect your man to
think or feel like a woman. He is wired differently, on purpose, by God. You need to know that in a man's mind, if
you love him, you will give him respect and honor. If you
love him, you will honor him enough to submit to his lead-
ership. This is the heart of God. Jesus, in His love for His
bride, the church, gave Himself unreservedly by laying

down His life for her. God, in His love for His children, makes sure they have every provision they need. We in return honor, praise, worship, and submit to God. God responds to our adoration and submission by pouring out even more of Himself and His blessings on us.

Also keep in mind that God is the only one who embodies both the emotions of man *and* woman because we were created in His image. Therefore, He has imprinted these distinct guidelines of love and respect to create balance between us in accordance with our makeup emotionally, spiritually, and physically. This is the order and cycle of love. However, sometimes a wedge is driven into the wheel, and we stop moving forward smoothly. We get stuck on disappointment, anger, resentment, unforgiveness, or disrespect, and we cut off the flow of love. A woman who does not respect her man usually loses her desire for him and finds it hard to submit to his need for intimacy, whether physical or emotional. As she holds her love and respect for silent ransom, he begins to struggle with his desire to give to her as he should. Thus the vicious cycle begins of love going downhill with no one quite knowing how to get it back on track.

Knowing and understanding what the other person needs are the first steps to moving forward. The other two are: Don't let the sun go down on your wrath; decide to love anyway. Why? Because God said so! Remember that one of the definitions of love is it does not keep a record of wrongs. What trouble would we all be in if God chose to keep a running tally of how we offend Him in thought, word, and deed on a daily basis. I shudder at the thought. Those who hold on to offenses, pressing them down inside and absorbing the acid that comes from unresolved pain and anger, will manifest them in other ways—this is the silent killer of many.

So what am I saying? If you are not married, this is the

time to examine the man you are considering and make the determination if this is a man you can respect and submit to. If not, do both of you a favor and leave him alone—for his sake, as well as your own. If you are married, you have a choice to make. Reach out and try to heal the great divide by speaking the truth in love to your man. Tell him what you need from him. As he responds to your words, praise and encourage him. Let him know what he is getting right and gently tell him what he needs to adjust. Remember, he is not a mind reader. If he does not or cannot respond, consider if he is able. This is more difficult, but you might have to just love him anyway as unto the Lord and trust God to begin to do in his heart what you could not do in his mind.

Sometimes a deeper work of healing must take place in that man in order for him to be what he needs to be for you. In some cases you need to take responsibility for the man you chose to marry. He is what he is and that cannot excuse you from the covenant you made with him. The good news is there is always hope, and the power of love has amazing transformation properties.

The bottom line is this—A man feels like a failure if he does not have the respect of his woman. If he feels like a failure, he will not fight and fuss; he will simply abdicate his responsibilities toward you or go in search of someone or something that makes him feel as if he is a success. You figure it out. But if you, oh woman, would give him the respect he so desperately needs, crowning him king on a daily basis, he will pull out all the stops to make you feel like a queen. And every diva knows it is more blessed to give than it is to receive simply because there is no way you can disrupt the law of reciprocation. You will get far more than you give.

ATTITUDE CHECK

Consider your current relationship. On a scale of one to ten, how respected do you make your mate or significant other feel?

What has kept you from honoring him as you should?

Why did you fall in love with him at first?

What has changed? What were the contributing factors?

What steps can you take to nurture him into the man you first fell in love with?

Diva Confession

Today I choose to show love to my partner by honoring him. I will find ways to show my respect, including _____.

Diva Devotion

Dear heavenly Father, make me a channel of Your love. Teach me how to walk in reverence before my mate, honoring him as I choose to honor and submit to You. May our relationship be a reflection of Your love to others. In Jesus' name, amen.

Diva-tude:

BE SACRIFICIAL

> And live a life of love, just as
> Christ loved us and gave himself
> up for us as a fragrant offering
> and sacrifice to God.
>
> EPHESIANS 5:2

What is the hardest part of being loving?

In what ways do you feel you are always called to sacrifice in your relationships?

What could the life lessons be that God is trying to make clear to you through these repeat occurrences?

Which of your requirements for love can you sacrifice for the sake of loving more fully?

What happens when you give of yourself with no thought of receiving? How do you feel when you make others feel loved?

Eighteen

Now that you have purified yourselves by
obeying the truth so that you have sincere love
for your brothers, love one another deeply,
from the heart.

1 PETER 1:22

The word *purity* is interesting. When we think of the
definition for it, we envision one who is clean, pristine, and
chaste. However, one of the definitions given for *purity* in
the Hebrew actually means "temple prostitute." Can you
believe that? But wait, don't get too excited. This was based
on the understanding that temple prostitutes were set apart
for the demands of their gods. When we are set apart for
the demands of our God—our heavenly Father—we, too,
will walk in purity, totally walking in the Word of His truth.
Doing things His way. In essence, loving deeply from the
heart, giving all we are and have without reservation.

When I think of God giving simply because it is His
nature to give, I'm quite humbled. If we are honest, most
of us give to get and become disgruntled when the one we
love, the one we are reaching out to, does not reach back
or respond the way we want him (her) to. Yet God gave
to a world that He knew would, for the most part, not
respond to His love, His sacrifice, His Word. Still, He gave

purposefully, willingly, sincerely, deeply, extravagantly, purely. Out of His holiness, He gives.

Now holiness is not just about being pure. The word also implies being whole. Perhaps this is the most overlooked secret to loving purely. If we are whole, perfect and entire, lacking nothing in ourselves, we won't rely on the love of others to make, validate, and affirm us. Loving will become an entirely pleasurable experience simply because it is what delights God. It delights Him because we are then reflecting His character in its purest form. God is holy because He is complete in and of Himself. He needs nothing else in order to be who He is. You cannot add to Him or subtract from Him. He doesn't change because He doesn't have to. He is already perfect, mature, complete, spectacular...all that He can be He already is! *Whew!* That is mind-blowing! The great "I Am" is already all that He can be, and there is no room for improvement. Because of this, He can love us with agape love—pure unconditional love. When we become complete in Him, we can love others with His love because we too are totally complete, needing nothing else.

For the married woman, this is good news. She can be a conduit of God's love to her mate and rock his world because she is free enough to love him into greatness without making her own demands. She stops intellectualizing his shortcomings and chooses to love him sincerely from the heart. Ladies, let me tell you, if you can achieve this, you will have that man addicted to your love forever. If you can make him feel as if he is growing into someone greater because of your love, as if he contributes something to your world that makes you smile, as if your love adds spice and variety to his life, he will bend over backward for you in every way, falling over himself to please you and serve you. And you will love him all the more for it. A married diva must return to her first love for her husband regularly in order to bring refreshing to her marriage. It is in the first flush of love that we love the hardest, the deepest, the strongest. Never let life's experiences rob you of the memory of why you first fell in love with your husband. If you can cling to that, you will automatically do what you did to get him in the first place, which was love him purely.

Single ladies, this is also good news for you because if you can be whole inside of God's love, it will free you from the angst of singlehood. You, my friend, will become a love magnet because the desperation will be gone and the love that radiates from you will draw others to you. This could present a problem because you will then have to pick which man you want! This is a good problem to have. The other thing living inside God's love will provide for you is the patience to exercise discernment and make better choices when it comes to men. Because you are already whole in Christ, you can take or leave anything or anyone who presents himself to you. This puts you in the driver's seat of your heart—in control and free to walk in purity as a woman set apart for the demands of her God. Now you can be a sister to the other men in your life. Every man you meet no longer has to be a potential husband. They can be brothers or friends whom you choose to love purely from the heart. Every diva knows the greatest gift she can give to the world is love that comes from a pure place without anything else attached to it because she has set aside her own demands to walk in truth according to the demands of her God. And yes, the truth will indeed make you free. Dare to love sincerely, deeply, and purely just because.

ATTITUDE CHECK

In what ways have you been set apart for your own desires?

How do your desires sometime take precedence over what God desires for you?

In what ways do you fail to feel whole? What do you think is lacking?

What do you feel God needs to do in you in order for you to feel complete?

If you didn't have to rely on anything or anyone other than God in order to feel whole, what would that do to your joy level? Your peace? Your security? Your ability to love others?

Why is it important for God to be the basis of your wholeness?

Diva Confession

Today I choose to love with a different attitude. I will love deeply, sincerely, and purely. I will reflect this by _____.

Diva Devotion

Dear heavenly Father, for far too long I have been sidetracked by my own demands and desires. Today I'm changing that and giving myself totally to You. As I choose to walk in truth according to Your desires, fill my heart with Your love that I might love as sincerely and deeply as You do. In Jesus' name, amen.

Diva-tude:

BE CONSIDERATE

> Finally, all of you, live in
> harmony with one another; be
> sympathetic, love as [sisters], be
> compassionate and humble.
>
> 1 PETER 3:8

How harmonious are your relationships?

What is the source of disharmony in your relationships?

What types of things stir your compassion? What cuts it off?
How can your attitude be different in those moments?

How does humility come into play with being compas-
sionate and sympathetic?

How can humility promote harmony in your relationships?

Nineteen

If anyone has material possessions and sees his
brother in need but has no pity on him, how
can the love of God be in him?

1 JOHN 3:17

We've all done it—been walking down the street
and heard that famous line, "Do you have some spare
change I can have?" And more often than not, we've chosen
to say, "No." Too jaded by the schemes of con men, too
suspicious of crafty alcoholics and drug abusers, we choose
not to donate to their habits. Some of us, if we are really
honest, have even thought in the back of our minds, "Get
a job!" Yet every now and then, something tugs at your heart
and tells you, "Give this one something." And so you turn
back and catch up to the one you automatically passed and
press a few bills into his hand. "God bless you!" he says
with tears welling up in his eyes. "God bless you." The
words echo in your spirit, and your heart swells because
you responded to God's voice to do something for someone
who could do nothing for himself at that moment.

I have been the recipient of the sanctimonious phrase,
"I'll pray for you," when I was in a tough financial place. I
have also been the recipient of monetary blessings from

people who were not my close friends, just people who were part of the family of Christ being moved by my heavenly Father to respond to my need in a tangible way. It is in those moments that my certainty of God's love and faithfulness has blossomed in my heart and drawn me closer to Him as I wonder at His constant care. It caused me to be more determined than ever to become who He wants me to be. We are the physical arms of God, and if we forget that, we lose out on perhaps the greatest opportunities to reflect Christ to the world. It is not enough to stand by voicing our concern for those who have pressing needs. God adjures us, in the words of a friend of mine, Audrey Ashe, "For God's sake, do something!"

One of the reasons God gives is so we can give. We have missed the purpose of all the getting if we miss this important fact. John says it best: "How can the love of God be in you if you choose to do nothing for someone less fortunate than yourself?" (1 John 3:17). The words of Mother Teresa came to me as I pondered this. She commented once, after someone commented on the poverty of the destitute in India, that she found those who had plenty to be poorest of all. She spent her life reaching out to those in need. Yet many, in a race to preserve their own comfort, disregard the discomfort of others.

I think of Tabitha (also called Dorcas) in the book of Acts, chapter 9, who sewed garments for the poor. After her death, folks gathered to mourn for her and so moved was Peter the apostle by their dedication to this precious, benevolent woman, that he prayed to God for her...and she was raised from the dead! It is our works that will outlast our lives, so do something that will last in the lives of others. The purest expression of love is that of giving with no thought of yourself, only of the need of the one before you. In this way, you become the arms of God to the lost, the goodness of God to those who simply need another burst of faith to make it through their trials. Perhaps it is the fear of their pain becoming ours that causes us to cut off people in need sometimes. The fear that their hardship could be contagious. Yet God encourages us to embrace their pain for His sake. Remember this, my friend, there will always be someone worse off than you, as well as some better off than you. Sow generously so that you might reap generously should need ever arise in your own life.

ATTITUDE CHECK

In what ways do you choose to be a conduit of God's generosity?

In what areas could you expand your giving?

What other things can you offer to those in need besides money?

How is God's love expressed to others when you give?

Why does this make God's love more of a reality in those moments?

What character traits are being built in us through our giving?

Diva Confession

I choose to be a channel of God's care by addressing the needs of those who cross my path and beyond. I will give out of the abundance that God has given to me because _____.

Diva Devotion

Dear heavenly Father, as You have given to me, so let me give to others that I might be an extension of Your loving care to them. Help me to overcome any preconceived ideas or fears that hinder me from being more giving. Free me to give from the heart as I follow Your instructions to make You real to others. In Jesus' name, amen.

Diva-tude:

BE GENEROUS

> Dear children, let us not love
> with words or tongue but with
> actions and in truth.
>
> 1 JOHN 3:18

How do we sometimes spiritualize our way out of doing something tangible to address the needs of others?

In what areas can we choose to move beyond our comfort zone to reach out to the needy?

What organization can you become personally involved with to be an instrument of God's care to others?

How are those in our midst affected by our care and giving?

Why is it necessary to be giving?

Twenty

Above all, love each other deeply,
because love covers over a multitude of sins.

1 PETER 4:8

*L*ove has been said to do many things. It'll make you do right when you want to do wrong. It'll make you sell the world for the good thing you've found. It will make you see harsh reality through rose-colored glasses. Certainly it made Shrek look like a prince to the princess. Truly love covers a multitude of sins, including a deficiency in good looks! How do we get past the irritations and annoyances that are sure to arise in relationships? By loving deeply. As we see people through the eyes of love versus through our expectations of them, we will be released to walk in love even when they are being unlovable.

It is through the eyes of love—through the eyes of Jesus—that God chooses to have compassion on us even when we are being totally undesirable and offensive to Him. His love covers our sins. We are told to forgive others and render mercy because the same measure we mete out will be given back to us by God. How can you refuse to forgive when God chooses to forgive you time and time again? The questions we must ask ourselves are, How deep is my love really? and, Am I willing to dig even deeper? Certain trees and plants, when encountering dry ground, force their roots deeper in search of water. Our hearts must seek to love deeply by digging deeper into the recesses of God's grace in search of more love to cover the things that threaten to separate us from others.

"But how do we love deeply when others hurt us deeply?" you may ask. Love looks beyond the fault and sees the need. Love doesn't take things personally. It recognizes the things that are broken in the other person and covers them. Jesus hanging on the cross, being kicked by onlookers while He was down, chose to forgive and pray for the forgiveness of those who were being disgustingly heartless. Loving deeply allows us to sympathize with the weaknesses and fears of others. At the root of every offense is a fear… remember that. Even pride comes from fear—the fear that we are secretly not as great as we would like to be.

A true diva knows that love is neither foolish nor weak. It takes strength to love, and courage to love deeply in spite of the response or lack of response from others. These are not things she tries to muster on her own. She relies on the grace of God empowering her love in the face of those who are undeserving. And instead of running for cover, she turns and covers someone who is shivering from the lack of love.

ATTITUDE CHECK

What areas do you struggle with when it comes to loving others?

How can you cover a loved one who is being unlovable?

How is God's love reflected through you when you love those who are being unlovable?

How can you reach past how you feel to embrace how God would like you to respond when your love is challenged?

In order to stay in the right attitude, what confession can you write for yourself when you are tempted to react rather than love?

Diva-tude:

BE FEARLESS

> And so we know and rely on the love God
> has for us. God is love. Whoever lives in love
> lives in God, and God in him. In this way,
> love is made complete among us so that we
> will have confidence on the day of judgment,
> because in this world we are like him. There is
> no fear in love. But perfect love drives out
> fear, because fear has to do with punishment.
> The one who fears is not made perfect in love.
>
> 1 JOHN 4:16-18

What do you fear the most when it comes to love? Why?

What things rob you of your confidence when you approach
God in prayer? How is your faith affected?

What do you believe about God's love for you? What is your
scriptural basis?

How does your inability to forgive yourself affect your
ability to forgive others?

Write a faith confession that will help you override your fears and increase your love.

Diva Inventory

On a scale of one to ten, how do you rate in the following attributes? (One being needs work; ten being great.) Write out a faith statement designed to hold yourself accountable to growth.

____Obedience

____Forgiveness

____Mercy

____Authenticity

____Integrity

____Fruitfulness

____Sacrificial

____Considerate

____Generosity

____Fearlessness

What can you do to increase in these areas?

Part 3

Overcoming

FINISHING WELL

For everyone born of God overcomes the world.

1 JOHN 5:4

The Ability to Thrive

hy aren't you married?" the woman asked me. In days of old, this question would have leveled me. I would have felt like a failure. I would have felt less than, incomplete, naked. But today I stood unmoved as I faced her with the dawning of a new revelation. Being married was the least of my worries. Mastering the accomplishments of the day was paramount for me, and right now, I was addressing a group of people, speaking truth into their lives that would hopefully bring about transforming change for the good in them. If I completed this one task, I will have done my job for the day and would be no less complete than any married individual because I had finished all that God required of me for the day.

It is the small, well-won victories in life on a daily basis that make us accomplished and complete in life. This is the understanding that every diva must grasp in order to be an overcomer. We have been called to do more than survive, to drag ourselves over the finish line. Yes indeed, we have been called to thrive in whatever circumstance we find ourselves planted in. I've said it often...a tree does not get to pick where it is planted, but it grows anyway.

Marriage is not an accomplishment. It is yet another leg on the journey toward refinement. (And an optional one at that.) Some of us will simply drive in different vehicles. Riches are not an accomplishment. There are many poor who are far richer because of their character, not their wallets. Fame and success are not accomplishments either, just telltale impressions marking the path where we walk. And let the record show that some have had a long run of it and finished poorly, fading into oblivion after being at the top of their game. A lot can happen between now and when we all finish; therefore, we must set our sights on more lasting fare. The only thing that will truly be an accomplishment is finally standing before Jesus with a crown, hopefully encrusted with more gems than we can lift. And this is one accomplishment we will not be able to claim credit for. In the end, the only way we truly overcome is by the blood of the Lamb and the confession of our faith. All other work done between here and eternity should be done with one thing in mind—to glorify God. As a diva sets her sights on purposeful living with this end in mind, she not only thrives and soars, she triumphantly overcomes.

Twenty-One

So God created man in his own image, in the
image of God he created him; male and female
he created them. God blessed them and said to
them, "Be fruitful and increase in number; fill
the earth and subdue it. Rule over the fish of
the sea and the birds of the air and over every
living creature that moves on the ground."

GENESIS 1:27-28

What are we all here for anyway? The answer is
quite simple and has never changed. We all come into the
world with the same mandate: to reflect the creative power
and benevolent love of our heavenly Father and Creator.
How do we do that? By being fruitful. As we exude the fruit
of the Spirit to others around us, it should cause them to
thirst for what we have, to want to meet God and become
more like Him. That is what being a Christian is all about.

We are called to be lights in the world and overtake the
darkness; to increase in number and influence so evil will
be subdued. We have been given dominion over all living
things as well as spiritual wickedness in high places. As we
use our God-given authority on the earth, as well as in the
spirit, we fulfill our call to occupy the earth victoriously until

Jesus comes again. We are, in a sense, His ambassadors—
His peacekeepers on a mission from God. Jesus was very
clear on why He was here. He stayed focused and finished
His assignment with flying colors. As an imitator of Him,
we, too, must complete our task with the same level of commitment. That will come in different forms for each one of
us. Because each part of the body is necessary, you and the
contribution you make will never be counted as small in
the kingdom. Looking at the big picture, it is clear to see
why each function and part of the body is necessary. No
task is insignificant because every little thing contributes to
the whole. The absence of one little toe can throw an entire
body off balance. From the garbage man to the master
inventor, every person is needed to do what he or she does
for the betterment of the whole. Now that you've done most
of the internal work, take the time to clarify your mission
and then get busy. I'll fill in the first two blanks for you.

Company name: Me, Myself, and I Unlim-
                       ited

Partner and CEO: Jesus

Product:

Service offered:

Company goal:

Customer base:

**On a scale of one to ten,
rate customer satisfaction:**

Areas that require improvement:

The measure of my success:

What are you passionate about?

How can your passion be channeled into a service that blesses others?

How does what you do affect God's reputation? The lives of others?

In what ways do you feel needed by others? What action does their need provoke from you in response?

How does meeting the needs of others bless you?

Diva Confession

I realize I am not here to simply please myself.
With this in mind, I will be about the business of
fulfilling my destiny and purpose. I will move
beyond my comfort zone and stretch my limits
beyond business as usual in my life today by

_____.

Diva Devotion

Dear heavenly Father, forgive me for focusing on
my own desires and wishes for far too long.
Restore a sense of mission in my heart. Write Your
mandate for me on my heart in such a way that
I can never escape it. Please empower me to do
what You have created me to do, and grant me
the grace to complete it. In Jesus' name, amen.

Diva-tude:

BE PURPOSE DRIVEN

"My food," said Jesus, "is to do
the will of him who sent me
and to finish his work."

JOHN 4:34

When do you feel a sense of accomplishment most?

What issues or needs in the world make you angry? Sad?

What is your favorite thing to do?

What assignment do you feel God has given you?

How will you go about accomplishing it?

Twenty-Two

I raised you up for this very purpose, that I
might display my power in you and that my
name might be proclaimed in all the earth.

ROMANS 9:17

n the end, remember this one thing: Ultimately God
will get the glory. Even those who do evil will be used for
God's glory, to display the greatest of that opposite virtue,
which is unadulterated goodness, and the power of it to
overcome the darkness. What does God's power look like
when it is manifested in you? How does He get the glory
out of your daily interactions and actions? Simple. Every day
we are called to defy the odds of conventional wisdom,
decorum, popular opinion, mainstream philosophy, and
even "natural reactions." What sets us apart is how we
respond in any given situation.

Every display of God's power is not a spectacular one.
At the end of the day, when all the fireworks, earthquakes,
and windstorms are over, it is the still small voice that will
haunt us most. It can be the one whispered instruction that
turned the tide of one person listening to the clamor of the
masses versus responding to the voice of God in the midst
of a highly charged situation. The power of God is displayed

141

every time you keep your cool while others are losing theirs. It becomes apparent when, in crisis, you steal away and return with sound wisdom to navigate through the storm. It is obvious when you keep standing when everything indicates you should have caved in. It is resoundingly present every time you choose to walk in faith and not cave in to fear. It can be life-changing for others as the evidence of God's presence and care is manifested in your answered prayers. Every diva should know that she is a walking, talking, living example of God's power and grace. Like a fine garment, she wears it well, allowing it to draw others to her Creator.

ATTITUDE CHECK

What types of pressures cause you to act out of character?

How does God get the glory when you remain centered in the midst of trying circumstances?

What can you do to strengthen yourself and respond wisely in times that test your character and faith?

What is your end goal? What would you like others to say about you? About God?

How will you make that statement a reality?

Diva Confession

I will be more aware than ever of whom I represent in thought, word, and deed. In light of the fact that my life is the only Bible some people will read, the one statement I want them to see is _____.

Diva Devotion

Dear heavenly Father, I long to be a mirror reflecting Your power. Make me a stunning representation of Your glory. Help me finish my course well, in a way that leaves a profound statement of my faith and Your faithfulness for all to see. In Jesus' name, amen.

Diva-tude:

BE DILIGENT

> Therefore, my [sisters], be all the more eager to make your calling and election sure. For if you do these things, you will never fall.
>
> 2 PETER 1:10

How does your decision to achieve certain goals keep you on course in the face of temptations and distractions?

What have you been created and called to do?

What do you need to do to make that happen?

What things would threaten you being able to carry out the call on your life? How will you go about protecting the call on your life?

In what ways will you guard yourself against falling?

Twenty-Three

Whatever you do, work at it with all your heart,
as working for the Lord, not for men.

COLOSSIANS 3:23

*W*ho do you ultimately work for? Every diva in the workforce must remember that ultimately she works for God. That's right. In spite of that knuckle-headed boss you serve, you really work for the King of kings and the Lord of lords. So keep your eyes on the prize, my sister. In the end, your workplace will be better because of your presence in it. Pray for the company you work for. If it prospers, so will you. The moment you walk into the building, the bar is raised to a new standard. God's standard. You are a kingdom representative.

I think of the power of Daniel's witness in ole sinful Babylon. He refused to compromise himself with all the delicacies the king fed his staff to keep them malleable and complacent. Instead, Daniel and his buddies chose to stick to the diet God had set for them. Because of their steadfast allegiance to their heavenly Boss (though forced to serve an earthly one), God gave them wisdom and learning that was noticed throughout the kingdom. And Daniel was promoted

145

through the ranks even when the administration changed!
Now you know that is unheard of, and yet it happened
because of Daniel's determination to put God first—but not
in an obnoxious, "religious" way. He simply and quietly lived
out his faith by remaining prayerful and using the wisdom
God gave him to serve his unbelieving king well. When the
jealousy of others moved them to set him up for destruction,
they could find no fault to mar his record or come against
him. In the end, they had to devise a plan to challenge his
faith, but Daniel would not be moved even though it could
cost him everything. In the end, he was cast into the lions'
den because he would not stop praying. But because God
was his ultimate Boss to whom he remained faithful, God
protected Daniel and glorified Himself in the midst of the
whole situation. So much so that the king decreed everyone
should worship Daniel's God! Now that is what I call making
a splash in the marketplace!

Every diva has the opportunity to have the same effect
on those who surround her at work or wherever she goes.
Walking in grace and graciousness, quietly serving others as
unto God, leaves a lasting impression we cannot buy. And
trust me, if you serve the one you were created to serve—
God—in all things, He will pick up the tab and lavish you
with benefits no earthly institution could provide.

ATTITUDE CHECK

If you were literally working for God, what would change
in your work ethic?

How would this be apparent in the way you carried yourself at work or approached your tasks?

What don't you like about your boss?

How could your attitude change him or her?

What don't you like about your work?

What attitude shift could make your work more enjoyable?

Who have you been called to affect on your job? In what way? In what way is your job the conduit to you achieving this greater mission?

Diva Confession

Today I choose to serve with a new attitude—
being ever mindful of the fact that ultimately it is
God I work for. Keeping this in mind, I will
change my approach to my work by_____

_____.

Diva Devotion

Dear heavenly Father, forgive me for the times I
allowed my vision of serving You to be blurred
by humanity getting in the way. As I purpose to
put You first in my work and all other things,
return to me the joy of serving where I have been
planted in this season. In Jesus' name, amen.

Diva-tude:

BE FOCUSED

> The [woman] who plants
> and the [woman] who
> waters have one purpose,
> and each will be rewarded
> according to his own labor.
>
> 1 CORINTHIANS 3:8

Are you a planter or a waterer?

Why is your role important in the lives of those in your home? At work? Those you encounter in other activities?

In what ways can you plant good seed in other people's lives? How can you water the seeds that have been planted?

What fruit has been harvested in the lives of those you invested in?

What is the ultimate reward of being fruitful? How does this bless you? Others?

Twenty-Four

The LORD will open the heavens,
the storehouse of his bounty, to send rain
on your land in season and to bless all the
work of your hands. You will lend to many
nations but will borrow from none.

DEUTERONOMY 28:12

Life is a series of seasons. As Solomon sagely stated in Ecclesiastes, there is a purpose for every season under heaven. As we pray for God's provision, we should be mindful to pray for our ability to handle it wisely so He can trust us with more. The ultimate understanding for having wealth of any kind is that the goal is not to bless ourselves, but to be a vessel of God's provision to others. With this in mind, our priorities concerning His provision and gaining abundance should change.

God does not want anyone beholden to anyone or anything but Him. If our financial situation holds us captive, we are not as free as we ought to be to serve Him. Financial lack can make you a prisoner to your need as opposed to being a servant to the one who can provide for you.

It is God's preference to make you a lender and not a borrower. However, today's verse also suggests you have a part to play. There must be a season of you planting something for Him to water. It is the work of your hands that He will bless, not good wishes or dreams that have not been worked. The only difference between the successful person and the person who is not is one followed through on a plan.

Every diva writes down the vision for her life and gets busy putting the right elements into place to make it happen. There is a season for diligently digging up the ground, getting the seeds put in place, covering the seeds, and then gently watering and nurturing your dream to life. There is also a season of waiting while God does His work beneath the surface. It may look as if nothing is going on, but indeed there is. Roots are growing and developing, traveling down deep to take hold of their place so the plant cannot be moved. In the midst of this, a diva trusts and applies herself to all she can do and leaves the rest to God. She anticipates a rich harvest, and when it comes, she dispenses it well.

ATTITUDE CHECK

What is your attitude toward money? Are you faithful with your tithe and offerings?

Are you able to give in your lack as well as in your abundance?

In what areas could your financial condition improve?

What steps can you take to work toward making this happen?

What are your greatest financial fears? How can you safeguard against them happening?

What seeds are you planting in order to reap financial security in the future?

Diva Confession

Today I choose to change my focus and priorities concerning wealth and abundance. I will become a vessel of provision whom God can use. I will become a storehouse for those in need by
_____.

Diva Devotion

Dear heavenly Father, forgive me for considering all that I've gained to be mine alone. I long to be used as a vessel of provision by You. Teach me to be a wise steward of all You bless me with. Grant me the discernment to know who You want to bless through me and what You have provided. In Jesus' name, amen.

Diva-tude:

BE EXPECTANT

> God is not unjust; he will not
> forget your work and the love
> you have shown him as you
> have helped his people and
> continue to help them.
>
> HEBREWS 6:10

Do you believe God takes note of your work? In what way is this evident to you?

In what ways do you know you please Him in regard to how you care for others?

In what ways has God promised to reward those who care for others?

What work have you done that you know God will remember?

What is the greatest joy you receive from helping others?

Twenty-Five

Therefore, my dear [sisters], stand firm. Let
nothing move you. Always give yourselves fully
to the work of the Lord, because you know that
your labor in the Lord is not in vain.

1 CORINTHIANS 15:58

You may be wondering what exactly is the work of
the Lord for your life. After all, you are not in ministry, you
work nine to five, or you're an entrepreneur. I've got good
news for you: That is the work of the Lord for you. We were
all created to fill different posts on the earth and to ultimately glorify God in every walk of life. From the stay-at-
home mom to the receptionist, from the cleaning lady to
the high-powered executive, from the electrician to the CEO
of a Fortune 500 company, it is all the work of the Lord.
These jobs are all necessary functions that must be done. Is
one greater than the other? Actually, no, because if people
were missing from their roles for a long period of time, their
absence would be felt as certain tasks that affected more
than one person were left undone.

Sometimes the job you perform may feel as if it is a
thankless one, but rest assured that if you remain unmoved
by the attitude of others and ever mindful of the fact that
you really work for the Lord, you are guaranteed your work

is not in vain. God holds our efforts in constant remem-
brance and rewards them in due season. Some seasons
seem to go on forever, leaving you to feel dry and devoid
of expectation, but please know this is merely a season. A
season where God is testing you, growing you, and
strengthening you to endure and excel. Can you be consistent when there is no promise of change? This is a major
character issue, and only one of the things that God will
test us on. Every delay, every endless stretch of discipline,
and even disappointing setbacks are designed to reveal
what is really going on in our hearts and to purge everything
that is not of God to make room for more succulent fruit in
our lives. And with the bearing up, no matter what, God
brings rich rewards.

Every diva knows that the race is not necessarily won
by the swift, but the rewards are given to those who endure
to the end. Those who start off with a bang at the beginning of the various projects in life yet fizzle miserably when
put to the test disappoint not only God and themselves, but
the countless others watching. Everyone longs to see cham-
pions. Divas encourage others to believe the best is possible for them as well. For this reason we should always be
aware of the effect our lives have on those around us. As a
walking epistle, remain steadfastly on course, knowing your
reward is sure in its season.

ATTITUDE CHECK

How do you feel about your work?

Can you see how what you do makes life better for others?

In what ways can your job become a ministry that blesses others? What opportunities do you have to touch others where you work?

What would make all your work worth it in the end?

What do you think God is saying to you in this place? In what ways can you grow as you wait for change?

Diva Confession

Today I choose to keep my eye on the prize versus how I feel about my work. I will not be moved by less than favorable conditions or even my own disappointed expectations. Instead, I will

_____.

Diva Devotion

Dear heavenly Father, forgive me for my negative attitude toward my work. Help me remember that my work is another way to glorify You. To that end, empower me to always keep the big picture in mind and not be distracted by those things that would pull me off the path of blessing. Help me to honor You in all I do. To Your praise and glory and in Jesus' name, amen.

Diva-tude:

BE STEADFAST AND OBSERVANT

> There is a time for everything,
> and a season for every
> activity under heaven.
>
> ECCLESIASTES 3:1

What season are you in now, and what does that mean to you?

How do you handle the season of waiting, when no movement is evident?

Are you able to focus on the big picture while you are waiting? What does that picture look like? What should you focus on right now?

How is your ability to recognize the season crucial to what you get out of this period of time in your life?

What do you think needs to die in you during this time? Why?

Therefore, since we are surrounded by such a great cloud of witnesses, let us throw off everything that hinders and the sin that so easily entangles, and let us run with perseverance the race marked out for us.

HEBREWS 12:1

Twenty-Six

There are six days when you may work, but the
seventh day is a Sabbath of rest, a day of
sacred assembly. You are not to do any work;
wherever you live, it is a Sabbath to the LORD.

LEVITICUS 23:3

Have you ever wondered what God did on the seventh day when He rested? I believe He took the time to enjoy the scenery, smell the flowers, and celebrate the beauty of His creation. His pause for the cause was not due to exhaustion, but rather to the understanding that rest is just as crucial to productivity as busyness is. I think by taking the time to enjoy the tasks already completed, He fueled His creative energy. Perhaps it was from this place of reenergizing Himself again and again that all things beautiful burst forth. Maybe everything that He created was good because it was birthed from a heart that was beating with fresh passion.

Now if God took the time to rest, who are we not to? We are mere mortals attempting to be like God, yet doing a lousy job as we suffer from burnout more than ever. "Overworked and underpaid," many mutter. The last bit of enjoyment has been squeezed out of their jobs a long time ago, no matter how much they once loved them. Why? Many times it's because of a lack of rest. Coughing from exhaustion and fresh out of fuel, we drag ourselves over the finish line and go splat, feeling unappreciated for all our efforts. This is not God's design. A true diva knows that rest is just as divine as accomplishment because without it, we can only go so far.

The more rested we are, the more creative energy we possess and the more enthusiasm we have for the tasks at hand. We bear more fruit because we are not running on empty. We have taken the time to recalibrate our spirits, replenish our souls, refuel our bodies, and refresh our minds. It is from this place of rest that tasks get approached from a healthy place and inspiration is released, along with the energy needed to complete the assignment in record time. After a good rest, it can be surprising to see how little time it takes to do something that took much longer when we approached it from a weary place.

Yet the myths of supermen and superwomen prevail, pressuring many onward and upward. The Sabbath has become just as busy a day as any other, with everyone dashing to finish off errands before the work week begins all over again. Small wonder countless men and women wake up on Monday just as exhausted as they were on Friday! "Is there an end in sight?" you wonder. Yes, but it begins with taking the time to enjoy what God has blessed you with—taking stock of all you've already done. You need to celebrate the present accomplishments and even stop long enough to dream a fresh dream. And then the rest, my friends, will be history.

ATTITUDE CHECK

What is your attitude toward rest?

Do you feel challenged to live out the superwoman myth? In what ways?

What do you wish you could change about your schedule?

When do you perform at your best? How often do you take the time for rejuvenation? What are some activities that refresh and rejuvenate you?

In what ways does taking the time to rest become an act of discipline? What things will you have to say no to in order to establish a ritual of rest for yourself?

Diva Confession

I will accept the fact that I cannot be all things to all people. I will take the time to get my second wind. I will acknowledge the importance of rest and practice taking the time to nourish my soul and renew myself. In order to be better for myself, my work, and others, I will establish the ritual of rest in my life by _____.

Diva Devotion

Dear heavenly Father, forgive me for being disobedient and not heeding Your command to rest. Teach me how to release all that I cannot complete today and trust You to redeem the time in the days to come. But most of all, help me to rest in You concerning everything in my life as I rely on Your perfect timing to work all things to the good. In Jesus' name, amen.

Diva-tude:

BE REVERENT

"If you keep your feet from breaking the Sabbath
and from doing as you please on my holy day, if
you call the Sabbath a delight and the LORD's holy
day honorable, and if you honor it by not going
your own way and not doing as you please or
speaking idle words, then you will find your joy in
the LORD, and I will cause you to ride on the heights
of the land and to feast on the inheritance of your
father Jacob." The mouth of the LORD has spoken.

ISAIAH 58:13-14

What does your Sunday usually look like?

What things would you consider "doing your own pleasure"
rather than what God has commanded?

Do you find it hard to be still? Why? What pressures compel
you to avoid rest? Do you feel guilt when you take the time
to rest? Why or why not?

How do you respond to people when you are tired? Are
you able to maintain a joyful disposition when you are tired?

What can you now do to establish a routine of resting?

Twenty-Seven

Do not offer the parts of your body to sin,
as instruments of wickedness, but rather offer
yourselves to God, as those who have been
brought from death to life; and offer the parts
of your body to him as instruments of
righteousness.

ROMANS 6:13

istorically speaking, when Paul was addressing the Romans, he was speaking to them where they lived. In many cities where temples were erected to various gods, part of the ritual of worship involved sexual acts in honor of these heathen gods. Paul was introducing a new type of worship to these flesh-bound citizens by suggesting now that they had come to the knowledge and acceptance of Jesus Christ, their bodies belonged to God. They were to use their bodies in a different type of worship—with purity, righteousness, and acts of service. Paul encouraged them to offer their bodies as living sacrifices of service to God, walking out the good, acceptable, and perfect will of God in a way that would bring glory to Him and blessings to others.

There are other parts of the body to worry about besides those that express our sexuality. Everyone struggles with

some part, and Paul is asking us to put this into perspective. He wants us to see the various parts of our body as
instruments—tools that can be used for good or evil. Our
tongues are part of our body. We are not to offer ourselves
to ungodly conversation or stir up strife through our words.
Our hands can be used for acts of selfishness or charity.
Our feet can be swift to carry us to the wrong places in pursuit of things that are not edifying or they can usher us to
places that afford us the opportunity to be blessings to
others—carrying good news and good gifts.

Doing good is part of enjoying the new life we have
been given. The old way of doing things is dead and gone,
along with our old nature. Gone, never to rise again. As an
offering of gratitude to God, every diva makes herself available to be used for His purposes. She is set apart for His
desires, knowing that all she has to offer is herself and her
availability. This is her greatest act of worship and one that
is well pleasing to the God who gave His all to redeem her.

ATTITUDE CHECK

How do you use your body as an instrument of worship to
God?

How can it be a vessel that grieves God instead of blessing
Him?

What portions of yourself do you need to exercise more discipline over?

How do you use all that you have for good to bless others?

When do you feel God smile with pleasure at what you are doing?

Diva Confession

From this day forward, I will recognize that I am a valuable tool in the hand of my God and King. I will no longer allow myself to be used for anything that does not bring glory to Him. As I examine my actions of the past, I now see that I must stop _____.

Diva Devotion

Dear heavenly Father, please forgive me for allowing myself to be used in ways that do not honor You. I surrender to Your lordship today. I offer my entire being to You as an act of worship. Teach me to walk before You in a way that continually honors You and blesses others. In Jesus' name, amen.

$\mathcal{D}$iva-tude:

BE RIGHTEOUS

> Flee the evil desires of youth, and
> pursue righteousness, faith, love
> and peace, along with those who
> call on the Lord out of a pure heart.
>
> 2 TIMOTHY 2:22

In what ways can you begin to take mastery over your desires?

What attitudes and responses can you adjust to help you pursue peace more?

In what ways have you offered parts of your body to un-righteousness in the past?

What do you now do differently?

Why is it important to pursue righteousness at this point in your life? What are the benefits?

Twenty-Eight

Above all else, guard your heart, for it is
the wellspring of life. Put away perversity from
your mouth; keep corrupt talk far from your
lips. Let your eyes look straight ahead, fix your
gaze directly before you. Make level paths
for your feet and take only ways that are firm.
Do not swerve to the right or the left;
keep your foot from evil.

PROVERBS 4:23-27

Though God promises to cleanse us from all unrighteousness, certain responsibilities are given to us to make right choices in life. In His fairness, God is faithful to reveal to us the root of where all good and bad choices originate.

God will not do all the work for you. It has always been His intention that you, as a free agent, be empowered by His Spirit to live above the law of sin as you make intelligent choices to safeguard your victory. First, let's begin by dealing with your heart.

We are led by our hearts. The heart is the throne room, the "hard drive" of our lives, so to speak. Consider us as complex computers. Whatever has been downloaded into our systems is manifested in our output—our attitudes, our words, and our actions. This is why we are instructed to be careful, to guard against "viruses." These can be wrong thoughts, beliefs, or programs coming in from the outside world that don't line up with the Word of God. Don't be deceived. What you embrace you will become.

Second, guard your lips. What comes out of them actually goes down into your soul. If they are negative, they fester. Ever notice when you share something that made you upset, you get even more upset? Mmm hmm, you are literally eating your own words, and they are becoming part of your system. Words that spread strife and confusion keep you off balance. You will literally eat the fruit of your own words! Make sure your words are pure and sweet, not bitter or nasty.

Third, be careful what you focus on. The "eye-gates" are vital. If your eye is full of light, then you will be full of light; the alternative is darkness. What goes in through the eyes goes to the mind. The eyes can deceive us in more ways than one. By now we know that appearances are one thing, living a life of faith is another. In the struggle with the flesh, the eyes often follow after what they see—choose what you focus on carefully. Continue to look straight before you, to the Author and Finisher of your faith. He has promised to guide you with His eye. As you keep a single-minded focus, He will lead you toward the light and the right path.

And last but not least—watch your walk. There is a shaky path and a sure one. It just makes sense to choose the path that is firm—one that will not give way, let you down, or sell you out. You wouldn't align yourself with a shaky person on purpose, so why take a path that is not secure? Focus on your destination. The path to victory is a sure one, well traveled and made sure by the promises of God, as well as by the faithfulness of all who have dared to be obedient to Him and refused to move on their own human impulses.

In a world filled with endless choices, every diva knows

there is a tried-and-true way to reap the right results for her life. She embraces the discipline of exercising the power she has been given to set sure boundaries for herself that keep her heart, mind, body, and soul safe, secure, and "virus free." This is not done reluctantly or grudgingly because she knows her life depends on it. Ultimately she is responsible for the life she has chosen to lead.

ATTITUDE CHECK

Which area(s) of temptation do you have to guard against the most?

In which areas do you have a tendency to relax and be caught off guard? When does this usually happen?

What is the outcome in these moments of self-indulgence?

What boundaries can you put in place in your life in order to exercise discipline?

What mindset do you need to adopt in order to embrace self-discipline with the right attitude?

Diva Confession

I will be more proactive than ever before in setting boundaries that secure my heart, my mind, and my being within the safe confines of God's plan for me. I will set myself on the path to victory by focusing on _____
and rejecting _____.

Diva Devotion

Dear heavenly Father, please forgive me for shirking my responsibility as the sentry of my heart and soul. As I redirect my focus, direct me and give me insight on the way that I should take. Raise up a standard against those things that threaten to dissuade me from the path You have chosen for me. Strengthen me for the journey so that I may finish victoriously. In Jesus' name, amen.

$\mathcal{D}$iva-tude:

BE SELF-CONTROLLED

> Therefore, [sisters], we have an
> obligation—but it is not to the sinful
> nature, to live according to it. For if you
> live according to the sinful nature, you will
> die; but if by the Spirit you put to death
> the misdeeds of the body, you will live.
>
> ROMANS 8:12-13

In what ways have you walked with a spirit of entitlement in the past?

When is it more tempting for you to feel as if you owe yourself a reprieve from God's guidelines for your life?

What has been the fruit of your departure from His instructions for your life?

What area in your life are you struggling most with now? How can you submit it to the control of the Holy Spirit?

Who can you walk in partnership with to hold you accountable?

Twenty-Nine

The mind of sinful man is death, but
the mind controlled by the Spirit is life and
peace; the sinful mind is hostile to God. It does
not submit to God's law, nor can it do so.
Those controlled by the sinful nature cannot
please God. You, however, are controlled not
by the sinful nature but by the Spirit,
if the Spirit of God lives in you.

ROMANS 8:6-9

Everybody has one, you know—a sinful or carnal mind, that is. It is part of our humanity, inherited from Adam. Until we allow our minds to be completely renewed by Christ, this sinful little factory inside of us produces thoughts and desires contrary to what God wants for us. It sees God as a cosmic killjoy whose rules and regulations make no sense. However, if we took the time to really realize what we truly want—life and peace—we'd know that's what God wants for us too. But the pull of our carnal flesh, which wants instant, "feel good" responses, wages war against the spirit, who longs to follow after and grow in God and do things His way. Sometimes we act based on what we feel we need at the time, and we become confused. If

175

we are not totally submitted to the Spirit of God and determined to exercise self-control no matter how deprived we might be feeling, we give in to those longings that have negative consequences. Finding ourselves deprived of the very peace we thought fulfilling the call of our flesh would give us, we return to God repentant—sometimes broken, but always worse for the wear.

The bottom line at the end of the day is when we walk in opposition to what God has instructed us to do, not only do we not please Him, our own pleasure is short-lived. The consequences of our choices and our actions come to steal the very peace and life we were seeking.

Here's the good news: You have a choice! Indeed, you do. You can choose to allow the Spirit of God to control you. You can relinquish control from your carnal nature to run your life and give it to God. It has always been God's will for you to have desires, not allow the desires to have you. There is a difference. Before knowing Christ, you had no choice—you were literally driven by your body, your mind, your heart, and your cravings. But the day you said "I do" to Jesus, He became the driver. Living in Him, you became the boss over your body and intentions. You get to say yes or no to every temptation that pulls and beckons your flesh to participate in things that are not profitable to your soul or your life.

This is called life mastery. The Spirit of God gives you the opportunity to master yourself and your mind. You get to decide your own boundaries and limitations that set the stage for victorious living. Focus and corral your inclinations. Lift and separate the good from the bad and become a "thinking Christian." No more over-spiritualizing life, but actively making decisions based on what you know God wants. With the help of His Spirit, you can now walk joyfully in your decision and expect good fruit.

Divas know they have the power to choose death or life,

blessings or curses, daily. No longer driven by any force but that of the Holy Spirit, they rejoice in making the right choice—to live at peace with God. To live a life that is pleasing to Him and ultimately pleasurable to them. With no more enemies because of conflicting desires, divas rest in the peace and life that come from actively submitting to the Spirit within instead of the flesh. They accept God's Word as good and true and see the merit of living an obedient life. This is the key to victorious living. After all, it has never been what you know, but Who you know. It's all about the relationship.

ATTITUDE CHECK

What would your attitude toward your body be if you practiced the awareness of the Holy Spirit residing inside of you?

What would you do differently? What would you begin to do? What would you stop doing? Why?

How would you evaluate your ability to make right choices for yourself? In what area are you more susceptible to making wrong ones?

What can you do to corral your focus and inclinations? What things or people can you put in place to help you with this?

What disciplines or reminders can you put in place to stay on track?

Diva Confession

I will no longer allow myself to be controlled by my desires. Instead, I will yield to the Spirit of God, who is my empowering partner. I will exercise my ability to choose life and victory for myself on a daily basis by _____.

Diva Devotion

Dear heavenly Father, I choose to be a friend and not an enemy. I invite You, Holy Spirit, to be my Partner and Helper. Show me the path ordained for me, and strengthen me to walk it in a way that brings pleasure to You and life to me. In Jesus' name, amen.

Diva-tude:

BE YIELDED

Do you not know that your body is a temple
of the Holy Spirit, who is in you, whom
you have received from God? You are not
your own; you were bought at a price.
Therefore honor God with your body.

1 CORINTHIANS 6:19-20

What should the temple of God look like?

Are you mirroring that physically?

In what better ways could you maintain your temple? How
will that honor God?

How have you perceived the value of your body? What is
the value of your body to God?

How will you begin to honor your body and God more
today?

Thirty

Yet a time is coming and has now come when
the true worshipers will worship the Father in
spirit and truth, for they are the kind of
worshipers the Father seeks.

JOHN 4:23

*E*very diva has hopes and dreams, but if becoming a true worshiper is your focus in life, you will do well. Every single aspiration you have can come to light if you do this one thing. True worshipers are grounded in the knowledge of what is truly important. As they seek the King and His kingdom, all other things are added to them because their spirits continually pursue God, and they live in the truth of His Word. It is the outpouring of their worship. The victory they possess is the reflection of a surrendered heart as God rewards their faithfulness. Their souls prosper from walking in a continual spirit of worship.

What does that worship look like? It is not simply the lifting of hands and the singing of a really good song. It is living the Word as God has spoken it. It is saying "yes" to the Spirit and "no" to the flesh 24/7, not just on Sunday morning or during midweek service. It is walking out what has been received in your inner woman through your divine connection to your heavenly Father. Being the living proof

181

that His Word works. Being a reflection of the Most High by living above the standards of the world.

Worshipers set the bar high and maintain it on the strength of their yieldedness. Actively submitting to God puts them in the position to be promoted by Him. God is seeking those He can trust to lift up, to elevate, to light up as beacons on a hill for the world to see. They are living witnesses of the power that is released through the empowering decision to worship the one true God.

Want to be healthy, wealthy, and wise? Accomplished? Secure? At the top of your game? Admired by your peers? All of our temporary goals will pass away in the light of the one thing that will remain through time—our acts of worship. They will speak for us as we stand before God. They will shine as gold. Our acts of worship will manifest themselves in gleaming jewels set in the crowns we will cast at the feet of Jesus. The only thing that truly matters is our worship.

ATTITUDE CHECK

What is truly important to you physically? Emotionally? Spiritually?

What is your favorite personal expression of worship?

How do your values line up with God?

Which of your goals are temporal? Which ones are eternal?

In what ways are you a living witness of God's glory, power, and faithfulness?

Diva Confession

In view of eternity, I will keep my priorities straight. I will make being a true worshiper my highest goal as I seek to produce fruit that will remain and bless God. In light of this determination, I realize that certain things are not so important, including _____.
Instead, I will shift my focus to _____.

Diva Devotion

Dear heavenly Father, I long to be a true worshiper, a person who brings pleasure to Your heart and reflects Your glory in a way that draws others to You. Teach me and lead me by Your Spirit and Your Word into all truth that I might render to You what Your heart seeks. In Jesus' name, amen.

Diva-tude:

BE A TRUE WORSHIPER

For it is we who are the circumcision, we who
worship by the Spirit of God, who glory in Christ
Jesus, and who put no confidence in the flesh....What-
ever was to my profit I now consider loss for the sake
of Christ. What is more, I consider everything a loss
compared to the surpassing greatness of knowing
Christ Jesus my Lord, for whose sake I have lost all
things. I consider them rubbish, that I may gain
Christ....Not that I have already obtained all this, or
have already been made perfect, but I press on to take
hold of that for which Christ Jesus took hold of me.

PHILIPPIANS 3:3,7-8,12

How can you balance earthly gains with your heavenly com-
mission?

What has been in first place in your heart?

How have wrong priorities kept you from achieving what
you wanted?

What would make it easier for you to follow God's leading
in this area?

What must you now do to master the discipline of being a
true worshiper?

Diva Checklist

On a scale from one to ten, honestly evaluate your level of exercising the following attributes of worship. Write the reason why you are not stronger in each particular area. Write three things that hinder you from being better in these areas and three steps you can take toward becoming stronger in these areas.

___ Purpose-driven

___ Diligence

___ Focus

___ Optimism

___ Steadfastness

___ Observant

___ Reverence

___ Righteousness

___ Self-control

___ Yieldedness

Finally, my sister...

Be spiritual. But not as the world displays it. No folding of the arms and humming to yourself for you! Instead, be spiritual in thought, word, and action. The apostle James said that being spiritual was feeding the widows and orphans. Avoid being so proud of your relationship with God that you are "religious" and ineffective for His sake.

Be spiritual, my sister, by being a walking conduit of God's love. Overcome evil with good. Remember, possessing diva-tude means disarming drama, not adding to it. Most of all, it's about being faithful. Faithful to the call that God has placed on your life. If you study to make your calling and election sure, you will never fail.

So live, love, give, and worship to your fullest potential, girl. God's got your back. Don't let trouble and trial get you down—it's all part of the journey of living, loving, and overcoming. On second thought, it's just part of the journey when you're a natural born diva! Until next time...

Love always,
Michelle

For more information on how you can attend a Diva Principle Conference near you, log on to:

thedivaprinciple.com
or
michellehammond.com

*"It's all about you so
you can be great for others!"*

OTHER BOOKS BY

Michelle McKinney Hammond

To contact Michelle or to book her
for a speaking engagement, log on to

michellehammond.com
or call
866-391-0955